For day hikers, section hikers, and thru-hikers

PACIFIC CREST TRAIL

Mileages, Landmarks, Facilities, Resupply Data, and Essential Trail Information for the Entire Pacific Crest Trail, from Mexico to Canada

DATA BOOK

6th Edition

Compiled by
Benedict "Gentle Ben" Go

 **WILDERNESS PRESS** . . . *on the trail since 1967*

千里の みちも いっぽから。

The Journey of a Thousand Ri begins with the first step.

Pacific Crest Trail Data Book

1st EDITION 1997
2nd EDITION 2000
3rd EDITION 2001
4th EDITION 2005
5th EDITION 2013
6th EDITION 2021
   2nd printing 2022

Copyright © 1997, 2000, 2001, 2005, 2013, 2021 by Benedict Go and Keen Communications LLC

ISBN 9780899979014 (pbk.); ISBN 9780899979021 (ebook)

Cartography: Scott McGrew
Cover photo: Section H in Southern California © Jordan Summers
Interior photos: page v, Benedict Go; page 127, top left: Laura Randall; page 127, center left, bottom left, top right, and bottom right: Jordan Summers
Calendars, pages 117–124: tashechka/Shutterstock.com

Published by (R) WILDERNESS PRESS
An imprint of AdventureKEEN
2204 First Ave. S., Ste. 102
Birmingham, Alabama 35233
800-678-7006, fax 877-374-9016

Manufactured in the United States of America
Distributed by Publishers Group West

Visit wildernesspress.com for a complete listing of our books and for ordering information. Contact us at our website, at facebook.com/wildernesspress1967, or at twitter.com/wilderness1967 with questions or comments. To find out more about who we are and what we're doing, visit blog.wildernesspress.com.

NOTICE: The author and publisher caution users of the data contained herein that land and resource managers along the route of the PCT can, and often do, make changes to the trail's routing, thereby changing or invalidating the information. Post offices and resupply points may be closed for numerous reasons at any time, so verify mailing addresses before shipping supplies. While every attempt has been made to verify this data when this book went to print, contact the Pacific Crest Trail Association (PCTA) and local agencies for current conditions and recent changes.

Acknowledgments

I would like to thank Wilderness Press and the authors of the PCT guidebooks, Laura Randall and Jordan Summers, for permitting the use of the guidebooks as the basis for the creation of the *Data Book*. Thank you also to the PCTA for all it does for the trail, Ray Jardine for publishing his ideas in long-distance hiking, Cindy Ross for sharing her journal, Halfmile for the revised measurements, and various trail users and maintainers who provided feedback on this book. Send any changes or comments to Ben at thork_erin@yahoo.com.

From the Author: The Journey

It has been almost 25 years since I embarked on the most incredible journey of my life. Back then, I wondered what I would feel in the future and how the journey would influence my life, if at all. Well, the future is here, and I'd like to share a few of my thoughts with those who dream of doing a thru-hike of the PCT.

The lessons I learned about myself have been very helpful to me, especially as a father. The fundamental question of what I want to teach my kids, of what would undoubtedly shape their lives, is something that became clear as I hiked the trail. Living on the trail, we are surrounded by life everywhere, from the trees to the animals to the sweet sound of creeks. One learns to observe how life progresses from a seed to a small tree to having flowers, bearing fruit, and ripening. Just as the great poet Rainer Maria Rilke once wrote about individuals ripening, so too must we work hard to provide children with a place where nature can take care of them and protect them from growing up too fast. Just as nature-ripened fruit tastes the best, so too will a nature-ripened child become the most beautiful. If my kids become long-distance backpackers, I would be very happy, not because they would have accomplished something but because of the life lessons they will learn and the skills and mentality they will develop. The trail will teach them how to adapt and survive, and with these skills, I know I won't have to worry about them for the rest of my life. They will become resourceful enough to know what to do no matter where life takes them, and in the end, that is all that matters.

For myself, I can honestly say that the lessons I learned in doing the thru-hike still guide me to this day: I learned the importance of taking care of family and health. I learned the importance of not limiting yourself to what you know, of having empathy; I cannot emphasize enough to my kids how important having empathy is—more so than having knowledge, for without it, one cannot relate to other people.

The trail has a tendency to make one become emotionally, mentally, and physically balanced. If one of these aspects is way out of proportion—if you're emotionally broken, mentally struggling, or physically hurt—it will be a little difficult at first, but the trail in time will heal you. Nature heals everything as much as she can. In times of difficulties, a little fresh air helps, and a bit of prayer doesn't hurt either. While hiking the trail, I have seen and experienced many things that I thought could not be possible, perhaps miracles. It led me to have an unconscious habit of praying, of giving thanks, whenever I'm in nature.

In hiking the trail, I learned to trust my instincts more than my knowledge; instinct is nature's way of increasing your knowledge. The trail will be all new; the places will be fascinating; some hold unimaginable beauties, and others unknown dangers. The trail will take you to places that will make you happy and places that will scare you. During all of these moments, your instincts will keep you safe.

Everything, every goal, has its own time. Once you pass that time, it doesn't mean you can't achieve that goal, but it often becomes more difficult. Yes, the trail will always be here, but life can get complicated. We are creatures of nature, of Mother Earth, and we are given a brief moment to enjoy her gifts. These moments begin when we are born and end when we pass. In between are stages when certain things are best done; let your instincts guide your path.

Finally, in all journeys, there is an ending. It is probably the hardest part of the entire thru-hike of the PCT. Completing such a monumental goal can lead to loneliness, for there are few who can truly relate. Please be gentle with yourself and cry if you need to; know that you are not alone in crying. The ending is difficult but, to quote Rilke again, "we must hold to what is difficult," for it is the only way we grow. Embrace the solitude and these feelings.

Everyone has their own story about their thru-hike. Many have written books, and some have created videos. Some of those stories are difficult to tell. To this day, I still am not capable of writing down my feelings about the experience. Descriptive words fail. Poets may be able to succeed. To this day, we read plays and listen to music created by powerful people long gone. These are people who are not only able to transcend space but also time; I suppose it is as close to immortality as one can be.

I made this data book as a way to give back to the trail, in the hope that it would be protected for future generations. Back in 1996, there were perhaps about a hundred hikers, and I thought that was a lot. But now, hearing that there are thousands of hikers, I can only imagine what it is like. Giving back to the trail is my way of staying connected. To see the PCTA grow to become what it is now, to see the trail become protected more and more, is a privilege. A big heartfelt thank-you to everyone.

To the younger generations, folks will get old, and someday it will be your turn. I hope you will continue to protect this most beautiful and wonderful trail. Doing a thru-hike of the PCT is the most beautiful gift that anyone can receive. The memories, the feelings that once in a while rise, will always be with you. To the future!

—*Ben "Gentle Ben" Go, October 2020*

A note about my trail name: when I started on the PCT, I met many Appalachian Trail thru-hikers, most of whom had trail names. For two months, I hiked across Southern California with the veteran AT hikers, pondering what my trail name should be. We finally reached Kennedy Meadows and saw the movie *The Legend of Grizzly Adams.* Next thing I knew, my trail name, Gentle Ben, came into being, bestowed by the one and only Rude Dog.

Ben and Ada's kids, Darren (10) and Jaevin (5), happy and proud to be on top of Mount Whitney after 12 days on the trail

PACIFIC CREST TRAIL

CANADA

Vancouver

E.C. Manning
Provincial Park

North
Cascades

Stehekin

Skykomish

Seattle

Spokane

Snoqualmie
Pass

Olympia

WASHINGTON

White
Pass

Cascade
Locks

Portland

Salem

OREGON

Bend

Cascade
Summit

Ashland

Hyatt Lake

Seiad Valley

Castella

Old Station

Belden

Sierra City

Echo Lake

South
Lake Tahoe

Sacramento

Reds Meadow

Bishop

San
Francisco

Edison Lake

Independence

Lone Pine

Fresno

CALIFORNIA

Kennedy Meadows

Tehachapi

Mojave

Lancaster

Agua Dulce

Wrightwood

Big Bear City

Los
Angeles

Idyllwild

Warner Springs

Mount Laguna

CONTENTS

INTRODUCTION 1

California Snow Depth Measurements 2
    past snow depths

Heading and Code Definitions 6
    headings and codes used in the Resupply and Trail Data

Resupply Data 9
    summary of places where packages can be sent and an index to
    quickly locate trail information by using the mileages as the link

ON THE TRAIL

SOUTHERN CALIFORNIA 17
    trail information from the Mexican border to Kennedy Meadows

This section covers the desert portion of the Pacific Crest Trail.
Water is scarce. Start early, rest in the shade during the hottest
part of the day, and resume hiking until evening.

CENTRAL CALIFORNIA 42
    trail information from Kennedy Meadows to Belden

This section covers the Sierra Mountains. Water is plentiful.
Snow is everywhere. Be careful, especially going up the south
face of Mather Pass. Practice using an ice ax.

NORTHERN CALIFORNIA 62
    trail information from Belden to the California–Oregon border

This section covers the Cascade Mountains in California. Water is
not a problem except for the Hat Creek Rim area, which is the
longest waterless stretch along the Pacific Crest Trail

OREGON 78
    trail information from the California–Oregon border to the Oregon–
    Washington border

This section covers the state of Oregon. With all the volcanoes, it
has some of the best tasting water along the Pacific Crest Trail.
Cross the state before fire season starts.

WASHINGTON 97
trail information from the Oregon–Washington border to Canada

This section covers the state of Washington. Cold rain becomes common. To prevent heat loss, pack all lunches in pockets and hike without stopping until reaching the day's destination. If there is too much snow before you reach Canada, wait to see if second summer in October comes and try to get to Canada again.

CALENDARS 117
for 2021–2028, with each year's post office holidays

Pacific Crest Trail Association 125

Jane and Flicka Endowment Fund 126

INTRODUCTION

*T*he *Pacific Crest Trail Data Book* contains a summary of the entire Pacific Crest Trail (PCT), covering a distance of more than 2,650 miles from Mexico to Canada. The trail passes through three states: California, Oregon, and Washington. The PCT terrain varies from desert in Southern California to the mountains of the High Sierra in Central California to the Cascades in far Northern California and continuing through Oregon and Washington.

This book was created as an adjunct to Wilderness Press's PCT guidebooks for planning and tracking, as well as a quick reference on the trail. Trail information is comprised of landmarks listed as they occur in a northerly direction, from Mexico to Canada. For each landmark, the following information is given: the mileage between points; the mileage from the Mexico border; its elevation; available facilities (such as water sources and post offices); gradient, indicating steepness to the next landmark; and an occasional water alert when the next water source is more than 12 miles away.

This book provides:

- An easy calculation of distances between any two points on the trail
- A profile of the trail elevation changes
- Assistance in preparing for hiking sections of the trail or the entire trail (a thru-hike)
- Assistance in establishing daily mileage goals while on the trail
- The average angle of the trail in degrees between the previous landmark and the current landmark.

Information in this sixth edition was obtained using the 2020 editions of *Pacific Crest Trail: Southern California, Pacific Crest Trail: Northern California,* and *Pacific Crest Trail: Oregon & Washington.* It also includes updates and comments from various trail users, maintainers, and government agencies. It is not intended for use as a navigation tool, nor does it provide any description of the trail's environment. For more information about the trail, including topographic maps, consult the PCT guidebooks. The books are available from various outdoor equipment stores or Wilderness Press.

Pacific Crest Trail Association
1331 Garden Hwy., Ste. 230
Sacramento, CA 95833
916-285-1846
pcta.org

Wilderness Press
2204 First Ave. S., Ste. 102
Birmingham, AL 35233
800-678-7006
wildernesspress.com

CALIFORNIA SNOW DEPTH MEASUREMENTS

The following table contains snow depths at various points in California, measured around April 1 each year. The value 0.0 is used when data is not available. For an indication of the location of these various points:

- Bighorn Plateau is next to Mount Whitney, the highest point in the 48 contiguous states.
- Bishop Pass is at a junction between Mather Pass and Muir Pass.
- Piute Pass is at a junction just after Muir Pass.
- Tuolumne Meadows is in Yosemite National Park.
- Bond Pass lies just west of the PCT on the boundary of Stanislaus National Forest and Yosemite National Park.
- Deadman Creek is next to Sonora Pass.
- Upper Carson Pass is in the Lake Tahoe area.
- Lower Lassen Peak is by Lassen National Park.
- Shasta Region is around the Mount Shasta area.

Beneath each heading is a course number, which refers to the snow course number assigned by the Department of Water Resources (DWR) in California. For the latest information on these points, contact DWR via cdec.water.ca.gov/cgi-progs/snowQuery and use the course numbers. Below the course numbers are the elevations for these points, which are followed by the actual snow depths in inches starting with the year 1995. At the bottom of the table is an average of the snow depths at each point.

CALIFORNIA SNOW DEPTH MEASUREMENTS

Year	Bighorn Plateau (C# 250)	Bishop Pass (C# 222)	Piute Pass (C# 183)	Tuolumne Meadows (C# 161)	Bond Pass (C# 159)
	11,350	11,200	11,300	8,600	9,300
1995	96.4	157.3	162.1	106.5	204.8
1996	70.1	94.6	111.4	61.6	116.2
1997	68.4	92.0	110.9	61.5	107.8
1998	99.0	133.0	132.7	92.4	147.0
1999	32.6	66.5	77.1	57.5	115.1
2000	56.1	71.7	80.1	43.4	104.0
2001	36.7	59.3	57.7	32.0	63.6
2002	65.3	79.7	78.7	55.3	108.9
2003	49.1	72.9	70.8	42.8	87.4
2004	41.1	61.5	77.4	39.9	78.5
2005	90.1	113.1	110.0	94.0	153.4
2006	53.0	130.1	124.2	98.1	162.1
2007	20.0	39.7	51.1	19.6	52.9
2008	65.0	72.8	85.3	48.7	91.6
2009	59.3	70.7	82.0	58.6	110.0
2010	62.5	81.5	94.6	54.1	92.6
2011	106.0	132.9	129.0	105.0	175.5
2012	20.6	45.6	49.0	29.4	58.1
2013	27.0	55.2	61.0	34.0	75.8
2014	27.0	43.0	50.0	16.5	46.5
2015	6.5	23.0	28.5	0.0	31.0
2016	45.0	66.0	82.0	48.8	107.5
2017	112.5	133.5	141.0	106.5	178.5
2018	45.0	78.0	88.5	44.5	111.5
2019	101.5	126.5	125.0	90.0	166.0
2020	35.0	55.5	0.0	29.0	75.5
AVERAGE	**57.3**	**82.9**	**90.4**	**58.8**	**108.5**

CALIFORNIA SNOW DEPTH MEASUREMENTS

Year	Deadman Creek (C# 345)	Carson Pass (C# 106)	Lassen Peak (C# 047)	Shasta Region (C# 018)
	9,250	8,500	8,250	7,900
1995	141.9	149.4	276.2	197.4
1996	87.9	88.8	171.0	112.8
1997	86.3	66.1	136.0	110.6
1998	117.0	112.2	250.3	196.5
1999	82.7	108.5	194.8	152.0
2000	75.3	69.8	178.4	139.4
2001	57.6	42.0	109.1	88.9
2002	73.6	78.3	166.3	113.1
2003	64.1	55.0	185.7	150.7
2004	57.2	50.1	187.1	138.1
2005	124.8	112.0	173.8	61.1
2006	137.3	123.4	266.5	0.0
2007	50.2	45.5	112.1	77.1
2008	69.9	57.1	132.5	82.4
2009	73.8	70.0	146.8	94.9
2010	70.3	74.0	169.5	144.3
2011	138.5	134.1	242.8	0.0
2012	43.1	53.0	145.1	120.6
2013	57.0	46.5	140.9	100.5
2014	60.0	42.0	122.0	59.0
2015	17.5	0.0	91.5	74.5
2016	79.0	81.5	199.0	129.0
2017	143.5	116.0	243.5	172.0
2018	97.0	89.5	131.5	72.0
2019	119.5	135.0	238.5	145.5
2020	0.0	66.5	0.0	69.0
AVERAGE	85.0	82.7	176.4	116.7

Crossing the High Sierra

The High Sierra in California has always been the major barrier for doing a thru-hike of the PCT. If you intend to do a thru-hike, the following equation is provided as a simple way of estimating when to reach Kennedy Meadows, the beginning of the High Sierra, en route to crossing the Sierra. You will still encounter plenty of snow, but it should not be overwhelming.

Kennedy Meadows Day = June 1 + (snow depth at Bighorn Plateau divided by 3.5) **days**

Note that the snow depths at Bighorn Plateau for various years are provided on page 3. Using this equation, the day to reach Kennedy Meadows, starting with 2005, are:

Year	Equation	Result
2005	June 1 + (90 / 3.5) days = June 1 + 26 days	June 27
2006	June 1 + (53 / 3.5) days = June 1 + 15 days	June 16
2007	June 1 + (20 / 3.5) days = June 1 + 6 days	June 7
2008	June 1 + (65 / 3.5) days = June 1 + 19 days	June 20
2009	June 1 + (59 / 3.5) days = June 1 + 17 days	June 18
2010	June 1 + (63 / 3.5) days = June 1 + 18 days	June 19
2011	June 1 + (106 / 3.5) days = June 1 + 30 days	July 1
2012	June 1 + (21 / 3.5) days = June 1 + 6 days	June 7
2013	June 1 + (27 / 3.5) days = June 1 + 8 days	June 9
2014	June 1 + (27 / 3.5) days = June 1 + 8 days	June 9
2015	June 1 + (6.5 / 3.5) days = June 1 + 2 days	June 3
2016	June 1 + (45 / 3.5) days = June 1 + 13 days	June 14
2017	June 1 + (112.5 / 3.5) days = June 1 + 32 days	July 3
2018	June 1 + (45 / 3.5) days = June 1 + 13 days	June 14
2019	June 1 + (101.5 / 3.5) days = June 1 + 29 days	June 30
2020	June 1 + (35 / 3.5) days = June 1 + 10 days	June 11

HEADING AND CODE DEFINITIONS

The column headings and codes used in the Resupply Data and On the Trail sections follow. The example used in the explanation refers to the following entry:

Landmark	Facilities	Diff	S→N	Elev	Gra
Water Alert (↑): 23.3 m					
Cross Oak Creek via a steel bridge	w	7.2	558.2	4,070	-2.9
Water Alert (↓): 25.1 m					

Landmark

The Landmark column contains a brief description of the trail at this location. In the example above, the landmark is "Cross Oak Creek via a steel bridge."

Facilities

The Facilities column contains codes corresponding to features available at this location. In the example above, *w* means that this location has a water source. The codes and their definitions follow:

DIRECTION CODES

N North, direction toward the North Pole

S South, direction toward the South Pole

E East, direction from which the sun rises

W West, direction to which the sun sets

Combinations of these codes are also used to designate in-between directions, such as NW for northwest or SE for southeast.

FACILITY CODES

PO Post Office. Packages can be mailed to and from this office.

w Water source. Depending on the season and time of year, a water source may not have water. Visit pctwater.com for information.

G Groceries, stores, supermarkets

M	Meals, restaurants, deli
L	Lodging, hotels, motels
sh	Shower
r	Register
R	Road
m	Miles
,	Comma. Facilities separated by commas are in the same location. For example, "PO, w, G: 0.30 m N" means that the post office, water source, and grocery store are all located 0.3 mile north.
;	Semicolons. Facilities separated by semicolons are *not* all in the same location. For example, "w; G: 0.30 m SE; sh" means that the water source and shower are nearby while the grocery store is 0.3 mile southeast.

The facility column is also used to give alerts of distances to water sources. Depending on the season, water sources do dry up. The guidebooks contain more information on the dependability of these sources. Visit pctwater.com for the latest water conditions. The criterion for water alerts is when the next water source within 0.5 mile of the trail is more than 12 miles away. In the example on the opposite page, "**Water Alert** (↓): 25.1 m" means that the next nearby water source reading down (heading north toward Canada) is 25.1 miles away, while "**Water Alert** (↑): 23.3 m" means that the next nearby water source reading up (heading south toward Mexico) is 23.3 miles away. These mileages include the side trail distances from the PCT to the water source, accounting for the differences in mileage heading north or south.

Heading Definitions
DIFF

The Difference column contains the mileage difference between the previous landmark to the current landmark. In the previous example, "7.2" means that the steel bridge at Oak Creek is 7.2 miles from the previous landmark, the headwaters of Burham and Pitney Canyons.

S→N

The S→N column contains the miles using the PCT southern terminus at the Mexican border as mile 0.0 and heading north. The mileage is cumulative to allow easy computation of distances between any two points on the trail. In the example above, 558.2 means that the steel bridge at Oak Creek is 558.2 miles from the southern terminus.

ELEV

The Elevation column refers to the approximate elevation of the landmarks. In the previous example, 4,070 means that the steel bridge at Oak Creek is at an elevation of 4,070 feet.

GRA

The Gradient column shows the average angle of the trail in degrees between the previous landmark to the current landmark. In the example above, -2.9 means that the trail is going down at an average of 2.9°. If the number is positive, the trail is going up. A large positive or negative number indicates that that part of the trail is steep. As a general guideline, the PCT follows the "no more than 15° going uphill and no less than 15° going downhill" rule.

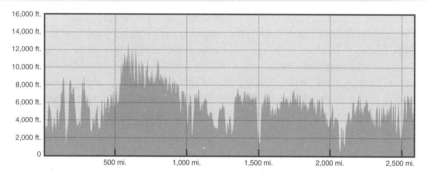

**Elevation Profile for the entire Pacific Crest Trail
from Mexico to Canada**

PCT TOTAL MILEAGE: 2,661.4 MILES

RESUPPLY DATA

Landmark	Facilities	Diff	S→N	Elev	Gra
General Delivery Campo, CA 91906 619-478-5466	PO, w, G, r, R: 0.30 m N	1.4	1.4	2,586	-1.9
General Delivery Mount Laguna, CA 91948 619-473-8341	PO, w, G, M, L, r, R: 0.40 m S	41.4	42.8	5,980	1.4
General Delivery Julian, CA 92036 760-765-3648	PO, w, G, M, L, r, R: 12.60 m W	34.5	77.3	2,252	0.1
General Delivery Borrego Springs, CA 92004 760-767-0741	PO, w, G, M, L, r, R: 18.70 m NE	0.0	77.3	2,252	0.1
General Delivery Warner Springs, CA 92086 760-782-3166	PO, w, M, r, R: 1.20 m NE	32.2	109.5	3,045	-2.7
Anza RV Resort Attn: (Your Name) PCT Hiker 41560 Terwilliger Road Space 19, Attn: PCT Anza, CA 92539 951-763-4819	w, G, sh, r, R: 5.80 m NW	33.6	143.1	4,075	-1.3
Paradise Valley Café Attn: (Your Name) PCT Hiker 61721 CA 74 Mountain Center, CA 92561 951-659-3663 theparadisevalleycafe.com for details	w, M, r, R: 1.00 m W	8.8	151.9	4,924	-2.6
General Delivery Anza, CA 92539 951-763-2074	PO, w, G, M, L, r, R: 7.00 m W	0.0	151.9	4,924	-2.6
General Delivery Idyllwild, CA 92549 951-659-1969	PO, w, G, M, L, sh, r, R: 4.50 m W	27.5	179.4	8,114	-3.9
General Delivery Cabazon, CA 92230 951-849-6233	PO, w, G, M, r, R: 4.50 m W	30.1	209.5	1,337	1.3
General Delivery Big Bear City, CA 92314 909-585-7132	PO, w, G, M, L, r, R: 5.40 m SW	56.6	266.1	6,830	0.1

Landmark	Facilities	Diff	S→N	Elev	Gra
General Delivery Big Bear City, CA 92314 909-585-7132	PO, w, G, M, L, r, R: 2.80 m SE	9.0	275.1	7,264	0.4
General Delivery Cedar Glen, CA 92321 909-337-4614	PO, w, G, M, L, R: 4.30 m SW	23.4	298.5	4,581	-1.7
Cajon Pass Inn Attn: (Your Name) PCT Hiker 8317 CA 138 Phelan, CA 92371; cajonpassinnphelan.com 760-249-6777 (call to confirm)	w, G, M, L, R: 0.60 m NW	43.5	342.0	2,995	-1.4
General Delivery Wrightwood, CA 92397 760-249-8882	PO, w, G, M, L, R: 4.50 m N	21.4	363.4	8,247	-0.8
Acton KOA Attn: (Your Name) PCT Hiker 7601 Soledad Canyon Road Acton, CA 93510 661-268-1214 $5 fee	w, sh, R: 0.20 m E	80.8	444.2	2,245	-3.7
General Delivery Acton, CA 93510 661-269-8618	PO, w, G, M, R: 5.80 m E	0.0	444.2	2,245	-3.7
General Delivery Lake Hughes, CA 93532 661-724-9281	PO, w, G, M, L, sh, r, R: 2.20 m NE	41.5	485.7	3,058	-2.9
Avangrid Renewables Attn: (Your Name) PCT Hiker 17890 Champagne Ave. Rosamond, CA 93560 661-256-2220, ext. 4321 (call to confirm) Via UPS or FedEx only!	w, R: 1.30 m E	51.2	536.9	3,465	2.3
General Delivery Tehachapi, CA 93581 661-822-0279	PO, w, G, M, L, r, R: 9.40 m W	21.6	558.5	4,150	2.7
General Delivery Mojave, CA 93502 661-824-3502	PO, w, G, M, L, r, R: 12.00 m E	0.0	558.5	4,150	2.7
General Delivery Onyx, CA 93255 760-378-2121	PO, w, G, r, R: 17.60 m W	93.5	652.0	5,264	3.0

Landmark	Facilities	Diff	S→N	Elev	Gra
Kennedy Meadows General Store Attn: (Your Name) PCT Hiker 96740 Beach Meadow Road Inyokern, CA 93527 559-850-5647 kennedymeadowsgeneralstore.com $6 fee	w, G, r, R: 0.70 m SE	50.2	702.2	6,009	0.2
General Delivery Lone Pine, CA 93545 760-876-5681	PO, w, G, M, L, r, R: 24.90 m E	43.1	745.3	10,492	1.3
General Delivery Independence, CA 93526 760-878-2210	PO, w, G, M, L, r, R: 24.00 m E	43.6	788.9	10,746	6.0
General Delivery Bishop, CA 93514 760-873-3526	PO, w, G, M, L, r, R: 33.30 m NE	42.1	831.0	8,751	2.1
Muir Trail Ranch Attn: (Your Name) PCT Hiker PO Box 176 Lakeshore, CA 93634; muirtrailranch.com	w 1.50 m NW; R	26.7	857.7	7,889	-1.1
Vermilion Valley Resort c/o China Peak Landing Attn: (Your Name) PCT Hiker 62311 Huntington Lake Road Lakeshore, CA 93634 559-259-4000; edisonlake.com Via UPS only!	w, G, M, L, R: 6.00 m W	21.0	878.7	7,877	-5.2
General Delivery Mammoth Lakes, CA 93546 760-934-2205	PO, w, G, M, L, r, R: 7.25 m NE	24.3	903.0	8,931	-1.0
General Delivery Tuolumne Meadows, CA 95389 209-372-4475	PO, w, G: 0.30 m SW; L: 1.30 m E; r: 0.30 m W; R	39.5	942.5	8,596	-1.0
Kennedy Meadows Resort and Pack Station Attn: (Your Name) PCT Hiker 42421 CA 108 Pinecrest, CA 95364 kennedymeadows.com Via UPS only!	w, G, M, L, sh, r, R: 10.20 m W	74.4	1,016.9	9,655	-3.3
General Delivery South Lake Tahoe, CA 96150 530-544-5867	PO, w, G, M, L, sh, R: 9.70 m NE	73.9	1,090.8	7,241	-2.0

Landmark	Facilities	Diff	S→N	Elev	Gra
General Delivery Meyers Post Office 1285 Apache Ave. South Lake Tahoe, CA 96150 530-577-5081	PO, w, G, M, R: 3.55 m NE	0.2	1,091.0	7,321	4.3
General Delivery Tahoe City, CA 96145 530-583-4900	PO, w, G, M, L, R: 12.00 m NE	33.8	1,124.8	7,658	2.7
General Delivery Olympic, CA 96146 530-583-5126	PO, w, G, M, L, R: 3.80 m E	14.6	1,139.4	8,086	5.0
Donner Ski Ranch Attn: (Your Name) PCT Hiker 19320 Donner Pass Road PO Box 66 Norden, CA 95724 530-426-3635; donnerskiranch.com	w, M, L, sh, r, R: 0.25 m W	14.0	1,153.4	7,114	2.9
General Delivery Soda Springs, CA 95728 530-426-3082	PO, w, G, M, r, R: 3.20 m W	0.0	1,153.4	7,114	2.9
General Delivery Truckee, CA 96161 530-587-7158	PO, w, G, M, L, r, R: 12.00 m E	0.0	1,153.4	7,114	2.9
General Delivery Sierra City, CA 96125 530-862-1152	PO, w, G, M, L, r, R: 1.50 m SW	42.0	1,195.4	4,591	-0.3
General Delivery Meadow Valley, CA 95956 530-283-1379	PO: 5.20 m E; w, G: 4.10 m E; R	72.5	1,267.9	5,518	0.0
Belden Town Resort and Lodge Attn: (Your Name) PCT Hiker 14785 Belden Town Road Belden, CA 95915 530-283-0570; beldentown.com Via UPS or FedEx only! $10 fee	w, G, M, L, R	19.0	1,286.9	2,254	4.8
General Delivery Chester, CA 96020 530-258-4184	PO, w, G, M, L, sh, R: 7.50 m NE	44.4	1,331.3	5,051	1.5

Landmark	Facilities	Diff	S→N	Elev	Gra
Drakesbad Guest Ranch Attn: (Your Name) PCT Hiker; include ETA 14423 Chester Warner Valley Road Chester, CA 96020 877-622-0221 (call to confirm)	w, M, L, sh, R: 0.25 m W	18.4	1,349.7	5,722	-1.5
General Delivery Old Station, CA 96071 530-335-7191	PO, w, G, M, L, sh, r, R: 0.30 m N	23.7	1,373.4	4,600	0.5
General Delivery Cassel, CA 96016 530-335-3100	PO, w, G, r, R: 1.50 m SW	33.9	1,407.3	2,990	-1.2
Burney Mountain Guest Ranch Attn: (Your Name) PCT Hiker 22800 Guest Ranch Road Cassel, CA 96016 530-335-2544 burneymountainguestranch.com for details	w, G, M, L, sh, R: 0.30 m SW	2.4	1,409.7	3,312	1.5
General Delivery Burney, CA 96013 530-335-5430	PO, w, G, M, L, sh, R: 8.00 m SW	1.6	1,411.3	3,112	-2.0
Burney Falls General Store Attn: (Your Name) PCT Hiker 24900 CA 89 Burney, CA 96013 530-335-5713 $7 fee	w, G, M, sh, r, R: 0.10 m E	7.7	1,419.0	2,944	-0.1
(Your Name) PCT Hiker c/o Ammirati's Market 20107 Castle Creek Road Castella, CA 96017 530-235-2676 (open when post office is closed)	w, G, R: 2.00 m SW	81.6	1,500.6	2,154	-4.6
General Delivery Castella, CA 96017 530-235-4413	PO, w, G, sh, r, R: 2.00 m SW	0.0	1,500.6	2,154	-4.6
General Delivery Dunsmuir, CA 96025 530-235-0338	PO, w, G, M, L, R: 4.50 m N	0.5	1,501.1	2,131	1.7
General Delivery Etna, CA 96027 530-467-3981	PO, w, G, M, L, R: 10.50 m NE	98.6	1,599.7	5,980	-6.1

Landmark	Facilities	Diff	S→N	Elev	Gra
General Delivery Seiad Valley, CA 96086 530-496-3211	PO, w, G, M, r, R	56.2	1,655.9	1,373	-0.1
General Delivery Ashland, OR 97520 541-552-1622	PO, w, G, M, L, R: 12.40 m N	56.0	1,711.9	6,054	-4.4
(Your Name) PCT Hiker c/o Callahan's Mountain Lodge 7100 Old US 99 S Ashland, OR 97520 541-482-1299; callahanslodge.com $5 fee	w, M, L, sh, R: 0.90 m N	6.8	1,718.7	4,207	-2.3
General Delivery Ashland, OR 97520 541-552-1622	PO, w, G, M, L, R: 12.90 m N	0.0	1,718.7	4,207	-2.3
Hyatt Lake Resort Attn: (Your Name) PCT Hiker 7900 Hyatt Prairie Road Ashland, OR 97520 541-482-3331; hyattlake.com Via UPS only!	w, G, M, sh, r, R: 0.75 m N	24.0	1,742.7	5,105	3.5
Fish Lake Resort Attn: (Your Name) PCT Hiker OR 140, Mile Marker 30 Eagle Point, OR 97524 541-949-8500; fishlakeresort.net	w, G, M, sh, R: 1.60 m W	30.5	1,773.2	4,952	-0.5
(Your Name) PCT Hiker; include ETA c/o Mazama Camper Store 700 Mazama Village Dr. Crater Lake, OR 97604 541-594-2255 Via UPS or FedEx only!	w, G, M, sh, R: 1.00 m SE	47.7	1,820.9	6,177	-1.4
General Delivery Crater Lake, OR 97604 541-594-3115 (call to confirm)	PO, w, G, M, L, R: 4.50 m NE	0.0	1,820.9	6,177	-1.4
General Delivery Crater Lake, OR 97604 541-594-3115 (call to confirm)	PO, w, G, M, L: 2.80 m SE	2.1	1,823.0	6,093	-1.5
General Delivery Diamond Lake, OR 97731 541-365-4411	PO, w, G, M, L, R: 5.60 m W	33.2	1,856.2	6,950	2.7

RESUPPLY DATA *(continued)*

Landmark	Facilities	Diff	S→N	Elev	Gra
Shelter Cove Resort Attn: (Your Name) PCT Hiker 27600 W. Odell Lake Road Crescent Lake, OR 97733 541-433-2548 Via UPS only!	PO, w, G, M, sh, r, R: 1.50 m SE	50.0	1,906.2	5,021	-2.8
Elk Lake Resort Attn: (Your Name) PCT Hiker 60000 Century Dr. Bend, OR 97701 541-480-7378 Via UPS or FedEx only! $5 fee	w, G, M, L, sh, R: 1.10 m E	46.4	1,952.6	5,250	-0.3
General Delivery Sisters, OR 97759 541-549-0412	PO, w, G, M, L, sh, R: 15.00 m NE	31.2	1,983.8	5,309	0.2
Big Lake Youth Camp Attn: (Your Name) PCT Hiker 26435 Big Lake Road Sisters, OR 97759 503-850-3562	w, M, sh, R: 0.70 m N	11.3	1,995.1	4,775	-3.3
General Delivery Government Camp, OR 97028 503-272-3238	PO, w, G, R: 6.00 m W	96.4	2,091.5	4,157	-2.1
Timberline Lodge Guest Services Attn: (Your Name) PCT Hiker 27500 East Timberline Road Government Camp, OR 97028 503-272-3158 $10 fee	w, G, M, L, sh, r, R: 0.10 m S	5.5	2,097.0	6,048	2.4
General Delivery Cascade Locks, OR 97014 541-374-5026	PO, w, G, M, L, sh, r, R: 0.25 m NE	49.6	2,146.6	229	-5.1
General Delivery Stevenson, WA 98648 509-427-5532	PO, w, G, M, L, sh, r, R: 2.70 m NE	0.6	2,147.2	192	-1.0
Trout Lake Grocery Attn: (Your Name) PCT Hiker PO Box 132 Trout Lake, WA 98680 509-395-2777 Via USPS	w, G, M, L, R: 13.60 m SE	81.7	2,228.9	3,849	-3.0

RESUPPLY DATA *(continued)*

Landmark	Facilities	Diff	S→N	Elev	Gra
White Pass Post Office (The Kracker Barrel Store) Attn: (Your Name) PCT Hiker 48851 US 12 Naches, WA 98937 509-672-3105 $5 fee	PO, w, G, M, sh, r, R: 0.70 m W	66.0	2,294.9	4,409	-5.2
Chevron Gas Station Attn: (Your Name) PCT Hiker 521 WA 906 Snoqualmie Pass, WA 98068 425-434-6688 $5 fee	w, G, M, L, R: 0.30 m SE	98.1	2,393.0	3,000	-1.0
Summit Inn Attn: (Your Name) PCT Hiker 603 WA 906 PO Box 163 Snoqualmie Pass, WA 98068 425-434-6300 $15 fee + tax if not staying	w, G, M, L, r, R: 0.30 m SE	0.0	2,393.0	3,000	-1.0
Stevens Pass Attn: (Your Name) PCT Hiker 93001 US 2 Skykomish, WA 98288 206-812-4510 Via UPS or FedEx only! stevenspass.com for details	w, M, R: 0.10 m W	71.1	2,464.1	4,053	-5.7
General Delivery Skykomish, WA 98288 360-677-2241	PO, w, G, M, L, r, R: 14.00 m W	0.0	2,464.1	4,053	-5.7
General Delivery Stehekin, WA 98852 509-682-2625	PO, w, G, M, L, sh, r, R: 10.60 m E	107.7	2,571.8	1,662	5.5

ON THE TRAIL

**Mile-by-mile trail data,
including landmarks, facilities,
cumulative mileages, elevations,
and trail gradients**

PACIFIC CREST TRAIL: Southern California

HUMBOLDT-TOIYABE
NATIONAL
FOREST

Las Vegas

Kennedy
Meadows
702.2 mi.

SEQUOIA
NATIONAL
FOREST

DEATH VALLEY
NATIONAL
PARK

NEVADA
CALIFORNIA

Walker
Pass

Onyx
652.0 mi.

MOJAVE
NATIONAL
PRESERVE

hachapi
8.5 mi.

Mojave
558.5 mi.

Rosamond 536.9 mi.

Barstow

Lake Hughes
485.7 mi.

Agua
Dulce

Acton
444.2 mi.

Cajon
Pass Inn
342.0 mi.

Cedar Glen
298.5 mi.

Big Bear City
266.1 mi.

ANGELES
NATIONAL
FOREST

Wrightwood
363.4 mi.

SAN BERNARDINO
NATIONAL
FOREST

Los
Angeles

Cabazon
209.5 mi.

JOSHUA TREE
NATIONAL
PARK

Idyllwild
179.4 mi.

Paradise
Valley Café
151.9 mi.

PACIFIC OCEAN

Anza 143.1 mi.

Warner Springs
109.5 mi.

ANZA-BORREGO
DESERT
STATE PARK

Salton
Sea

CLEVELAND
NATIONAL
FOREST

Julian
77.3 mi.

Mount Laguna
42.8 mi.

San Diego

UNITED STATES

MEXICO

Campo 1.4 mi.

20 miles

20 kilometers

SOUTHERN CALIFORNIA

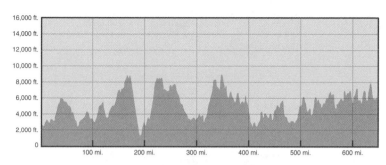

Elevation Profile for Southern California
From the Mexican Border to Kennedy Meadows

SEGMENT TOTAL MILEAGE: 702.8 MILES

Landmark	Facilities	Diff	S→N	Elev	Gra
Mexican border		0.0	0.0	2,918	0.0
San Diego Gas & Electric, cross a dirt road	R	0.3	0.3	2,805	-4.1
Cross another dirt road	R	0.3	0.6	2,710	-3.4
Cross Forrest Gate Road	R	0.1	0.7	2,707	-0.3
Three old concrete steps next to Forrest Gate Road	R	0.7	1.4	2,586	-1.9
General Delivery Campo, CA 91906 619-478-5466	PO, w, G, r, R: 0.30 m N	0.0	1.4	2,586	-1.9
San Diego & Arizona Eastern Railroad's tracks		1.6	3.0	2,464	-0.1
Creeklet, winter and early spring	w	1.4	4.4	2,380	-0.7
Pipe gate to little-used road	R	4.4	8.8	3,361	2.4
Another jeep road	R	0.2	9.0	3,343	-1.0
Cross east-descending jeep road	R	1.9	10.9	3,345	0.0
Viewpoint of Hauser Mountain		0.5	11.4	3,400	1.2
South Boundary Road 17S08	R	2.6	14.0	2,939	-1.9
Junction with a 1988-vintage trail segment		0.7	14.7	2,831	-1.7

SOUTHERN CALIFORNIA

Landmark	Facilities	Diff	S→N	Elev	Gra
Cross Hauser Creek, winter and early spring	w	0.7	15.4	2,317	-8.0
Saddle southeast of Morena Butte		1.3	16.7	3,190	7.3
Leave jeep trail		0.2	16.9	3,150	-2.2
Viewpoint north over the southern Laguna Mountains		1.0	17.9	3,495	3.7
Jeep road in a saddle	R	0.3	18.2	3,400	-3.4
Corner of Lake Morena Drive and Lakeshore Drive	w; G: 0.30 m SE; sh; R	1.8	20.0	3,074	-2.0
Ridgetop		1.4	21.4	3,220	1.1
Bridge over Cottonwood Creek, winter and early spring	w	2.7	24.1	3,065	-0.6
Cottonwood Creek, winter and early spring	w	1.4	25.5	3,107	0.3
Boulder Oaks Campground	w	0.5	26.0	3,183	1.6
Boulder Oaks Road/Old Highway 80	R	0.1	26.1	3,165	-2.0
I-8	R	0.5	26.6	3,145	-0.4
Kitchen Creek Road	R	3.6	30.2	3,995	2.6
Fred Canyon, creek usually dry		1.8	32.0	4,205	1.3
Fred Canyon Road 16S08	w, R: 0.80 m NW	0.6	32.6	4,409	-0.9
Long Canyon	w	4.3	36.9	5,195	2.6
Long Canyon Creek ford		1.1	38.0	5,435	2.4
Second road crossing	w: 0.30 m NW; R	0.8	38.8	5,889	6.2
Morris Ranch Road	R	1.1	39.9	6,005	1.1
South boundary of Burnt Rancheria Campground		1.6	41.5	5,955	-0.5
Spur to Burnt Rancheria Campground		0.6	42.1	5,971	0.6
Desert View Picnic Area	w	0.5	42.6	5,956	-0.3
General Delivery Mount Laguna, CA 91948 619-473-8341	PO, w, G, M, L, r, R: 0.40 m S	0.0	42.6	5,956	-0.3
Paved road leading to Stephenson Peak	R	0.2	42.8	5,981	1.4
Second paved road	R	0.6	43.4	5,915	-1.2

Landmark	Facilities	Diff	S→N	Elev	Gra
Dirt spur descending from highway, junction to Laguna Campground	w, sh, R: 0.70 m SW	4.1	47.5	5,422	-1.3
Trail junction, faucet southwest across Sunrise Highway S1 at Penny Pines	w, R: 0.12 m SW	1.2	48.7	5,433	0.1
Barren saddle	R	0.8	49.5	5,562	1.8
Saddle west of Garnet Peak		0.7	50.2	5,491	-1.1
Pioneer Mail Picnic Area, late spring and summer	w	2.4	52.6	5,274	-1.0
Water Alert (↓): 24.7 m					
Kwaaymii Point Road	R	0.8	53.4	5,472	2.7
Jeep road down to Oriflamme Canyon	R	1.4	54.8	5,250	-1.7
Another jeep road down to Oriflamme Canyon	R	2.9	57.7	4,875	-1.4
Second ridgetop	R	1.3	59.0	5,060	1.5
Faint jeep track above Oriflamme Canyon	w: 0.60 m W	0.5	59.5	4,996	-1.4
Mason Valley Truck Trail		2.9	62.4	4,694	-1.1
Upper Chariot Canyon, by a road junction, water 0.60–1.80 m N usually dry	R	1.3	63.7	3,864	-6.9
Mason Valley cutoff road	R	0.3	64.0	4,075	7.7
Cross a gap		2.6	66.6	4,240	0.7
Cross Rodriguez Spur Truck Trail, water 0.90–1.30 m W	w: 1.30 m W	1.8	68.4	3,653	-3.5
Rocky gap on Granite Mountain's north ridge		3.2	71.6	3,390	-0.9
Another gap		1.9	73.5	3,130	-1.5
Reach County Highway S2	R	2.9	76.4	2,255	-2.2
Cross County Highway S2	R	0.6	77.0	2,278	-5.0
Cattle gate next to concrete bridge, next to San Felipe Creek		0.1	77.1	2,257	-3.0
Water Alert (↑): 24.7 m					
Cross CA 78, San Felipe Creek, may be contaminated	w, R	0.2	77.3	2,261	0.1

SOUTHERN CALIFORNIA

Landmark	Facilities	Diff	S→N	Elev	Gra
General Delivery Julian, CA 92036 760-765-3648	PO, w, G, M, L, r, R: 12.60 m W	0.0	77.3	2,252	0.1
General Delivery Borrego Springs, CA 92004 760-767-0741	PO, w, G, M, L, r, R: 18.70 m NE	0.0	77.3	2,252	0.1
Water Alert (↓): 23.8 m					
Pipe gate, past the crest of San Felipe Hills		8.7	86.0	3,364	1.4
Dry, sandy wash		0.6	86.6	3,210	-2.8
Ridgecrest		1.6	88.2	3,596	2.6
East-branching jeep road	R	2.1	90.3	3,485	-0.6
Poor jeep road beyond a pipe gate	R	0.9	91.2	3,559	0.9
Cattle gate		2.6	93.8	4,141	2.4
Veer northeast through a gap		1.9	95.7	4,395	1.5
Water Alert (↑): 23.8 m					
Barrel Spring	w	5.4	101.1	3,482	-1.8
Montezuma Valley Road S22	R	0.1	101.2	3,453	-3.1
PCT post marking the crossing of a jeep road	R	2.1	103.3	3,285	-0.9
San Ysidro Creek	w	1.7	105.0	3,354	0.4
Cross a good dirt road	R	1.2	106.2	3,524	1.5
Cross ridgetop jeep road	R	1.4	107.6	3,510	-0.1
Bridge of two-lane CA 79	w, R: 0.20 m NE	1.9	109.5	3,045	-2.7
General Delivery Warner Springs, CA 92086 760-782-3166	PO, w, M, r, R: 1.20 m NE	0.0	109.5	3,045	-2.7
Recross jeep road	R	0.7	110.2	2,960	-1.3
Cross Agua Caliente Creek, usually dry		0.6	110.8	2,910	-0.9
Abandoned campground		0.4	111.2	2,926	0.8
Bridge under CA 79	w, R	0.2	111.4	2,929	0.1
Old jeep trail		0.6	112.0	2,960	0.6

SOUTHERN CALIFORNIA

Landmark	Facilities	Diff	S→N	Elev	Gra
Junction with a dirt road	R	0.2	112.2	2,965	0.3
End of dirt road	R	0.4	112.6	2,990	0.7
Agua Caliente Creek	w	2.1	114.7	3,189	1.0
Switchback in a side canyon		1.0	115.7	3,520	3.6
Lost Valley Road	R	2.4	118.1	4,170	2.9
Spur road past Lost Valley Road	w, R: 0.20 m NW	1.4	119.5	4,349	1.4
Water Alert (↓): 17.8 m					
Drop east to a saddle		3.0	122.5	4,945	2.2
Chihuahua Valley Road	R	4.8	127.3	5,057	0.3
Combs Peak		1.9	129.2	5,592	3.1
Tule Canyon		2.2	131.4	4,710	-4.4
Dirt road at the Anza-Borrego Desert State Park boundary	R	2.8	134.2	4,107	-2.7
Tule Canyon Creek		2.0	136.2	3,590	-2.8
Water Alert (↑): 17.7 m					
Tule Canyon Truck Trail	w, R: 0.25 m SE	0.8	137.0	3,620	0.4
Coyote Canyon Road	R	2.7	139.7	3,510	-0.4
Nance Canyon seasonal creeklet, early spring	w	0.5	140.2	3,347	-3.5
Water Alert (↓): 29.5 m					
Chamise-covered gap		2.1	142.3	4,185	4.3
Sandy jeep road	R	0.8	143.1	4,086	-1.3
Anza RV Resort Attn: (Your Name) PCT Hiker 41560 Terwilliger Road Space 19, Attn: PCT Anza, CA 92539 951-763-4819	w, G, sh, r, R: 5.80 m NW	0.0	143.1	4,086	-1.3
Table Mountain's shoulder		3.9	147.0	4,909	2.3
Alkali Wash		1.2	148.2	4,540	-3.3
Low pass across the flanks of Lookout Mountain		3.1	151.3	5,070	1.9

SOUTHERN CALIFORNIA

Landmark	Facilities	Diff	S→N	Elev	Gra
Pines to Palms Highway (CA 74)	w, M, R: 1.00 m NW	0.6	151.9	4,924	-2.6
Paradise Valley Cafe Attn: (Your Name) PCT Hiker 61721 CA 74 Mountain Center, CA 92561 951-659-3663 theparadisevalleycafe.com for details	w, M, r, R: 1.00 m W	0.0	151.9	4,924	-2.6
General Delivery Anza, CA 92539 951-763-2074	PO, w, G, M, L, r, R: 7.00 m W	0.0	151.9	4,924	-2.6
Penrod Canyon creek, usually dry		3.7	155.6	5,098	0.5
FS 6S01A	R	2.0	157.6	5,700	3.3
Saddle on Desert Divide, junction to Tunnel and Live Oak Springs	w: 1.00 m E	0.8	158.4	5,952	3.4
Cross private mining road		1.4	159.8	6,400	3.5
Climbers' trail to Lion Peak		0.7	160.5	6,600	3.1
Cedar Spring Trail 4E17 (alternate route)	w: 1.00 m N	2.1	162.6	6,775	0.9
Saddle		0.7	163.3	6,945	2.6
Fobes Ranch Trail 4E02 (alternate route)	w: 0.60 m SW	3.2	166.5	5,994	-3.8
Spitler Peak Trail (alternate route)		2.1	168.6	7,009	5.3
Water Alert (↑): 29.0 m					
Apache Spring Trail	w: 0.50 m E	0.6	169.2	7,352	6.2
Gap on San Jacinto's crest		2.9	172.1	7,200	-0.6
Above Andreas Canyon		3.4	175.5	8,380	3.8
Join Tahquitz Valley Trail	w: 0.33 m N	1.8	177.3	8,134	-1.5
Tahquitz Peak Trail 3E08		0.7	178.0	8,619	7.5
Saddle Junction		1.4	179.4	8,114	-3.9
General Delivery Idyllwild, CA 92549 951-659-1969	PO, w, G, M, L, sh, r, R: 4.50 m W	0.0	179.4	8,114	-3.9
Wellman Divide Trail		1.8	181.2	8,992	5.3
Strawberry Cienaga		0.9	182.1	8,597	-4.8

SOUTHERN CALIFORNIA

Landmark	Facilities	Diff	S→N	Elev	Gra
Deer Springs Trail 3E17		1.4	183.5	8,047	-4.3
Marion Mountain Trail		1.6	185.1	8,706	4.5
North Fork San Jacinto River, below Marion Mountain Trail	w	0.5	185.6	8,830	4.5
Fuller Ridge		2.0	187.6	8,725	-0.5
Fuller Ridge Trail		2.9	190.5	7,746	-3.7
Black Mountain Road 4S01	w, R: 1.30 m SW	0.2	190.7	7,663	-4.5
Switchback in dirt road	R	1.9	192.6	6,860	-4.6
Narrow gap	w: 0.20 m S	1.3	193.9	6,393	-3.9
Falls Canyon and One Horse Ridge Overlook		2.3	196.2	5,372	-4.8
View of Fuller Ridge		2.4	198.6	4,385	-4.5
Small saddle west of Knob 3,252		3.2	201.8	3,200	-4.0
Snow Canyon Road, water out of a fountain	w, R	3.9	205.7	1,730	-4.1
Falls Creek Road	R	1.3	207.0	1,235	-4.1
Snow Creek Road 3S01	R	0.1	207.1	1,230	-0.5
Cross jeep roads	R	0.7	207.8	1,195	-0.5
Cross a good gravel road	R	0.4	208.2	1,210	0.4
Join a good dirt road	R	0.7	208.9	1,265	0.9
I-10	R	0.6	209.5	1,337	1.3
General Delivery Cabazon, CA 92230 951-849-6233	PO, w, G, M, r, R: 4.50 m W	0.0	209.5	1,337	1.3
Second power line road	R	0.5	210.0	1,475	3.0
Buried Colorado River Aqueduct		0.4	210.4	1,580	2.8
Cottonwood Road	R	0.6	211.0	1,690	2.0
Cross two side-by-side roads	R	0.5	211.5	1,850	3.5
Gold Canyon Road	R	0.2	211.7	1,845	-0.3

SOUTHERN CALIFORNIA

Landmark	Facilities	Diff	S→N	Elev	Gra
Mesa Wind Farm	w, R	1.7	213.4	2,338	3.1
Narrow pass between Gold and Teutang Canyons		1.2	214.6	3,225	8.0
Teutang Canyon		0.7	215.3	2,815	-6.4
Canyon View Loop		2.4	217.7	2,746	-0.3
Old jeep road in Whitewater Canyon, close to Whitewater Creek	w, R	0.8	218.5	2,312	-5.9
PCT marker	w	1.8	220.3	2,610	1.8
Ridgetop		0.8	221.1	3,166	7.6
West Fork Mission Creek Road	R	0.6	221.7	2,918	-4.5
Veers from dirt road	R	0.2	221.9	3,010	5.0
East Fork Mission Creek Road	R	3.8	225.7	3,060	0.1
Cross East Fork Mission Creek	w	0.5	226.2	3,128	1.5
End of the dirt road next to East Fork of Mission Creek	w, R	1.0	227.2	3,360	2.8
Cross Mission Creek	w	4.9	232.1	4,834	3.2
Pleasant creek	w	3.4	235.5	6,128	4.1
Water Alert (↓): 20.7 m					
Jeep road built for logging		3.2	238.7	7,371	4.2
Meet FS 1N93 with MISSION SPRINGS TRAIL CAMP sign	R	1.2	239.9	7,928	5.0
FS 1N05	R	0.7	240.6	8,235	4.8
FS 1N05 crossing in a saddle	R	0.8	241.4	8,118	-1.6
Unpaved road east of Peak 8,828		3.3	244.7	8,490	1.2
FS 1N96	R	0.7	245.4	8,510	0.3
Cross Coon Creek Road 1N02	R	1.0	246.4	8,089	-4.6
Reach a perpendicular trail		1.5	247.9	8,610	3.8
Cross a dirt road	R	0.6	248.5	8,635	0.5
Cross a jeep road	R	0.5	249.0	8,390	-5.3

SOUTHERN CALIFORNIA

Landmark	Facilities	Diff	S→N	Elev	Gra
Better dirt road	R	0.3	249.3	8,387	-0.1
Four roads and a trail	R	0.7	250.0	8,100	-4.5
Junction		1.0	251.0	8,395	3.2
Dirt road just east of CA 38 and Onyx Summit	R	1.1	252.1	8,531	1.3
FS 1N01	R	1.1	253.2	8,636	1.0
Broom Flat Road 2N01	R	2.1	255.3	7,899	-3.8
Water Alert (↑): 20.7 m					
Arrastre Trail Camp at Deer Spring	w	0.9	256.2	7,605	-3.5
Spring	w	0.5	256.7	7,456	-3.2
FS 2N04	R	1.5	258.2	7,155	-2.2
Arrastre Creek Road 2N02	R	3.7	261.9	6,782	-1.1
CA 18	R	4.2	266.1	6,830	0.1
General Delivery Big Bear City, CA 92314 909-585-7132	PO, w, G, M, L, r, R: 5.40 m SW	0.0	266.1	6,830	0.1
Doble Road 3N08	R	2.0	268.1	6,855	0.1
Unsigned spur trail down to Doble Trail Camp	w: 0.13 m E	0.5	268.6	6,902	1.0
Second jeep road	w, R: 0.67 m N	4.1	272.7	7,688	2.1
Cross a better road	R	0.5	273.2	7,560	-2.8
Caribou Creek	w	1.7	274.9	7,257	-1.9
Van Dusen Canyon Road 3N09 next to Caribou Creek	R	0.2	275.1	7,264	0.4
General Delivery Big Bear City, CA 92314 909-585-7132	PO, w, G, M, L, r, R: 2.80 m SE	0.0	275.1	7,264	0.4
Bertha Peak, first jeep road	R	1.6	276.7	7,720	3.1
Bertha Peak, second jeep road	R	0.7	277.4	7,735	0.2
Cougar Crest Trail 1E22		0.3	277.7	7,674	-2.2
Polique Canyon Road 2N09	R	0.9	278.6	7,550	-1.5

SOUTHERN CALIFORNIA

Landmark	Facilities	Diff	S→N	Elev	Gra
FS 3N12, atop a saddle, junction to Delamar Spring	w, R: 0.90 m W	2.5	281.1	7,755	0.9
Cross a dirt road	R	0.9	282.0	7,610	-2.0
Cross a jeep road	R	1.1	283.1	7,305	-3.0
Little Bear Spring Trail Camp	w	2.5	285.6	6,577	-3.2
Holcomb Creek	w	0.3	285.9	6,502	-2.7
Reach a saddle		2.0	287.9	6,485	-0.1
Cross a dirt road	R	0.8	288.7	6,350	-1.8
Crab Flats Road 3N16	R	3.5	292.2	5,469	-2.7
Cross Holcomb Creek		0.2	292.4	5,430	-2.1
Cross Holcomb Creek again	w	0.8	293.2	5,331	-1.3
Cienega Redonda Trail, next to Cienega Redonda Fork of Holcomb Creek	w	0.2	293.4	5,325	-0.3
Hawes Ranch Trail	w	0.3	293.7	5,230	-2.6
Holcomb Crossing Trail Camp		0.4	294.1	5,215	-0.5
Bench Trail Camp	w	0.6	294.7	5,185	-0.5
Hawes Peak Trail		0.2	294.9	5,158	-1.5
90-foot steel and wood bridge spanning Deep Creek	w	3.6	298.5	4,581	-1.7
General Delivery Cedar Glen, CA 92321 909-337-4614	PO, w, G, M, L, R: 4.30 m SW	0.0	298.5	4,581	-1.7
Bacon Flats Road 3N20	R	2.8	301.3	4,263	-1.2
Deep Creek Hot Spring	w	6.6	307.9	3,522	-1.2
Cross Deep Creek via bridge		2.1	310.0	3,318	-1.1
Mojave Forks Dam (alternate route)		3.0	313.0	3,135	-0.7
Deep Creek ford	w	0.6	313.6	2,990	-3.1
CA 173	R	0.7	314.3	3,127	1.9
Little-used jeep road	R	0.4	314.7	3,205	2.1
Trailside spring (unreliable)		1.9	316.6	3,482	1.6

Landmark	Facilities	Diff	S→N	Elev	Gra
Turnoff to Mojave River Forks Regional Park	R	1.0	317.6	3,371	-1.2
Mojave River Forks Campground	w, sh, R: 0.75 m N	0.0	317.6	3,371	-1.2
Jeep road	R	0.1	317.7	3,411	4.3
Grass Valley Creek	w	0.3	318.0	3,331	-2.9
Steep jeep road	R	0.7	318.7	3,480	2.3
North-descending jeep road halfway to Silverwood Lake	w, G, R: 0.30 m NW	2.6	321.3	3,474	0.0
CA 173	R	2.5	323.8	3,166	-1.3
Very poor dirt road south of Mojave Siphon Powerplant	R	0.6	324.4	3,201	0.6
First saddle in Silverwood Lake State Recreation Area		0.6	325.0	3,460	4.7
Unsigned spur trail to Garces Overlook		2.5	327.5	3,580	0.5
Cross a jeep road	R	0.8	328.3	3,455	-1.7
Two-lane bike path to Cleghorn Picnic Area	w: 0.50 m E	0.4	328.7	3,392	-1.7
Signed junction to group-camp complex		0.1	328.8	3,380	-1.3
Silverwood Lake State Recreation Area's entrance road	w, G, M, sh, R: 1.70 m E	0.2	329.0	3,397	0.9
Off-ramp, west		0.1	329.1	3,395	-0.2
Small picnic area		0.4	329.5	3,468	2.0
Narrow paved road to water tank	R	0.4	329.9	3,530	1.7
Leave recreation area and join a jeep road	R	2.0	331.9	4,023	2.7
Road atop scenic Cleghorn Ridge	R	0.3	332.2	4,160	5.0
Small stream	w	0.9	333.1	3,829	-4.0
Little Horsethief Canyon's dry creekbed		2.5	335.6	3,587	-1.1
Road under a huge power-transmission line	R	2.5	338.1	3,840	1.1
Cross FS 3N44	R	2.3	340.4	3,350	-2.3
Cross another road	R	0.4	340.8	3,300	-1.4
Descending dirt road	R	0.2	341.0	3,165	-7.3

SOUTHERN CALIFORNIA

Landmark	Facilities	Diff	S→N	Elev	Gra
Better dirt road, end of descent	R	0.3	341.3	3,150	-0.5
Crowder Canyon	w	0.1	341.4	3,129	-2.3
Water Alert (↓): 28.9 m					
Road before I-15 in Cajon Canyon	R	0.6	342.0	2,995	-2.4
Cajon Pass Inn Attn: (Your Name) PCT Hiker 8317 CA 138 Phelan, CA 92371 760-249-6777 (call to confirm) cajonpassinnphelan.com	w, G, M, L, R: 0.60 m NW	0.0	342.0	2,995	-2.4
Railroad tracks		0.9	342.9	2,969	-0.3
More railroad tracks		0.2	343.1	3,013	2.4
FS 3N78, second power line road	R	1.2	344.3	3,335	2.9
Swarthout Canyon Road 3N28	R	3.0	347.3	3,568	0.8
Jeep road	R	0.4	347.7	3,685	3.2
Sharpless Ranch Road 3N29	R	4.1	351.8	5,195	4.0
Gap in the ridge		0.9	352.7	5,260	0.8
Sheep Creek Truck Road 3N31	R	3.5	356.2	6,293	3.2
Viewpoint on ridgetop flat		0.2	356.4	6,350	3.1
Road end just east of Gobblers Knob	R	0.8	357.2	6,480	1.8
Jeep road atop Blue Ridge	R	4.5	361.7	8,135	4.0
Posted trailhead to Mount Baldy		0.8	362.5	8,312	2.4
Acorn Canyon Trail		0.9	363.4	8,247	-0.8
General Delivery Wrightwood, CA 92397 760-249-8882	PO, w, G, M, L, R: 4.50 m N	0.0	363.4	8,247	-0.8
Guffy Campground		1.0	364.4	8,251	0.0
Dirt road beside an artificial lake	R	2.2	366.6	8,130	-0.6
PCT pathway on the west side of the reservoir		0.1	366.7	8,120	-1.1
East Blue Ridge Road 3N06	R	0.4	367.1	7,937	-5.0

Landmark	Facilities	Diff	S→N	Elev	Gra
Blue Ridge Campground		0.2	367.3	7,894	-2.3
Angeles Crest Highway (CA 2)	R	2.1	369.4	7,372	-2.7
Water Alert (↑): 28.9 m					
Grassy Hollow Visitor Center	w	0.9	370.3	7,310	-0.7
Spur to walk-in Jackson Flat Group Campground		1.1	371.4	7,480	1.7
FS 3N26	R	1.6	373.0	7,220	-1.8
Vincent Gap		1.0	374.0	6,582	-6.9
Side trail to Lamel Spring	w: 0.06 m S	1.7	375.7	7,768	7.6
Mount Baden-Powell Spur Trail		2.2	377.9	9,245	7.3
Spur trail to Dawson saddle		2.6	380.5	8,856	-1.6
Cross-country to Lily Spring	w: 0.33 m N	1.2	381.7	8,540	-2.9
Windy Gap		1.8	383.5	7,576	-5.8
Little Jimmy Spring	w	0.2	383.7	7,435	-7.7
Little Jimmy Trail Camp		0.2	383.9	7,479	2.4
Cross a dirt road/trail	R	1.1	385.0	7,360	-1.2
Angeles Crest Highway (CA 2)	R	1.0	386.0	6,666	-7.6
Mount Williamson Summit Trail		1.9	387.9	7,774	6.3
Angeles Crest Highway (CA 2)	R	1.4	389.3	6,700	-8.4
Eagles Roost Picnic Area (start of detour)		0.9	390.2	6,654	-0.6
Rattlesnake Trail 10W03		1.2	391.4	6,165	-4.4
Little Rock Creek	w	0.3	391.7	6,080	-3.1
Burkhart Trail 10W02 next to Little Rock Creek (detour rejoins PCT)	w	2.1	393.8	5,675	-2.1
Leave Burkhart Trail		0.2	394.0	5,721	2.5
Cooper Canyon Trail Camp	w	1.2	395.2	6,235	4.7
Climb to a gap east of Winston Peak		1.0	396.2	6,700	5.1
Dirt road to Cooper Canyon Trail Camp	R	0.7	396.9	6,645	-0.9

SOUTHERN CALIFORNIA

Landmark	Facilities	Diff	S→N	Elev	Gra
Headwaters of Cooper Canyon Creek	w	0.4	397.3	6,530	-3.1
Cloudburst Summit		0.7	398.0	7,032	7.8
Second highway crossing below a hairpin turn	R	0.8	398.8	6,733	-4.1
Road junction in Cloudburst Canyon	R	0.6	399.4	6,545	-3.4
Camp Glenwood Boy Scout Camp	w	1.2	400.6	6,252	-2.7
CA 2	R	0.5	401.1	6,268	0.3
Three Points Trailhead on Angeles Crest Highway (CA 2)	R	2.0	403.1	5,928	-1.8
Unused dirt road	R	1.5	404.6	5,760	-1.2
Another dirt road leads to a group camp	R	0.2	404.8	5,655	-5.7
Signed trail junction, hikers left, horses right		1.7	406.5	5,240	-2.6
Sulphur Springs Trail Camp	w: 0.20 m E	0.1	406.6	5,270	3.3
Merge with the foot trail		0.5	407.1	5,265	-0.1
Little Rock Creek Road 5N04	R	0.3	407.4	5,315	1.8
Gap at the head of Bare Mountain Canyon		2.4	409.8	5,830	2.3
Shaded Fiddleneck Spring	w	0.6	410.4	6,232	7.3
Fountainhead Spring	w	0.6	411.0	6,436	3.7
Ridgetop vista point		1.3	412.3	6,760	2.7
Shady gap near Mount Pacifico Campground		0.7	413.0	6,650	-1.7
Jeep road	R	1.6	414.6	6,380	-1.8
Trail resumes		0.4	415.0	6,210	-4.6
Signed spur trail to Pacifico Mountain Road 3N17 trailhead	w, R	3.5	418.5	4,980	-3.8
Mill Creek Summit	w	0.1	418.6	4,979	-0.1
Cross Mount Gleason Road	R	2.6	421.2	5,595	2.6
Signed side trail		3.1	424.3	5,640	0.2
FS 4N24	R	0.5	424.8	5,521	-2.6
Flat area just below the trail		1.0	425.8	5,195	-3.5

SOUTHERN CALIFORNIA

Landmark	Facilities	Diff	S→N	Elev	Gra
Junction with a south-branching trail		3.8	429.6	6,360	3.3
Mount Gleason's north ridge		0.4	430.0	6,410	1.4
Messenger Flats Campground	w	0.4	430.4	5,886	-14.0
Moody Canyon Road	R	1.5	431.9	5,375	-3.7
Santa Clara Divide Road	R	1.2	433.1	5,425	0.5
PCT tread resumes		0.1	433.2	5,395	-3.3
West-descending jeep track		0.7	433.9	5,395	0.0
BPL Road 4N32, North Fork Saddle Ranger Station	w, R	2.2	436.1	4,185	-6.0
Mattox Canyon Creek (unreliable)		4.1	440.2	2,685	-4.0
Cross Indian Canyon Road 4N37	R	2.9	443.1	2,619	-0.2
Soledad Canyon Road	R	1.1	444.2	2,245	-3.7
Acton KOA Attn: (Your Name) PCT Hiker 7601 Soledad Canyon Road Acton, CA 93510 661-268-1214 $5 fee	w, sh, R: 0.20 m E	0.0	444.2	2,245	-3.7
General Delivery Acton, CA 93510 661-269-8618	PO, w, G, M, R: 5.80 m E	0.0	444.2	2,245	-3.7
Flat just before Santa Clara River ford	w	0.1	444.3	2,226	-2.1
Railroad tracks		0.2	444.5	2,256	1.6
Saddle out of the canyon		0.4	444.9	2,485	6.2
Young Canyon Road	R	1.3	446.2	2,960	4.0
Gap near the head of Bobcat Canyon		0.7	446.9	2,780	-2.8
Jeep road separating Soledad and Escondido Canyons	R	1.6	448.5	3,160	2.6
Saddle during the descent		0.5	449.0	2,960	-4.3
Canyon bottom		1.9	450.9	2,400	-3.2
Antelope Valley Freeway 14	R	0.2	451.1	2,379	-1.1
Cross to the canyon's north side		0.8	451.9	2,335	-0.6

SOUTHERN CALIFORNIA

Landmark	Facilities	Diff	S→N	Elev	Gra
Vasquez Rocks trail junction		0.1	452.0	2,323	-1.3
Junction on dirt road, descending west	R	0.7	452.7	2,435	1.7
Gate at a large parking area		0.2	452.9	2,482	2.6
Escondido Canyon Road	R	0.7	453.6	2,482	0.0
Agua Dulce Canyon Road	R	0.4	454.0	2,470	-0.3
Darling Road (downtown Agua Dulce)	w, G, M, R	0.5	454.5	2,537	1.5
Old Sierra Highway	R	1.8	456.3	2,725	1.1
Mint Canyon Road	R	0.1	456.4	2,730	0.5
Petersen Road	R	0.2	456.6	2,755	1.4
Dirt road	R	0.1	456.7	2,755	0.0
Angeles National Forest boundary		0.4	457.1	2,905	4.1
Mint Canyon step-across creek		1.5	458.6	2,865	-0.3
Big Tree Trail 14W02		1.1	459.7	3,330	4.6
Martindale Ridge Road (FS 6N07)	R	2.6	462.3	4,500	4.9
Up to a low saddle		0.3	462.6	4,555	2.0
Bear Spring	w	0.6	463.2	4,331	-4.1
Water Alert (↓): 15.2 m					
Ridgetop-firebreak jeep trail		0.7	463.9	3,995	-5.2
Old PCT		0.6	464.5	3,785	-3.8
Bouquet Canyon Road 6N05	R	1.0	465.5	3,334	-4.9
Old California Riding and Hiking Trail (CRHT)		2.7	468.2	3,985	2.6
Pass with another firebreak above Leona Divide Road	R	1.3	469.5	4,300	2.6
Spunky Edison Road 6N09	R	2.0	471.5	3,747	-3.0
Ridge with a firebreak		2.2	473.7	3,815	0.3
Water Alert (↑): 15.0 m					
San Francisquito Canyon Road, water may be contaminated	w, R: 0.15 m SW	4.5	478.2	3,392	-1.0

Landmark	Facilities	Diff	S→N	Elev	Gra
Dirt road above San Francisquito Canyon	R	0.4	478.6	3,520	3.5
Grass Mountain Road	R	1.2	479.8	4,270	6.8
Saddle where four dirt roads converge	R	1.4	481.2	3,899	-2.9
Tule Canyon Road 7N01	R	1.3	482.5	3,900	0.0
Lake Hughes Road 7N09	R	3.2	485.7	3,058	-2.9
General Delivery Lake Hughes, CA 93532 661-724-9281	PO, w, G, M, L, sh, r, R: 2.20 m NE	0.0	485.7	3,058	-2.9
Trailside wet-season spring	w	1.4	487.1	3,734	5.2
Water Alert (↓): 17.5 m					
Sawmill-Liebre firebreak		0.7	487.8	4,190	7.1
Maxwell Truck Trail 7N08		2.1	489.9	4,530	1.8
Cross two dirt roads	R	3.0	492.9	4,680	0.5
Maxwell Trail Camp	R	0.1	493.0	4,643	-4.0
Ascend to a trail intersection with the closed Upper Shake Campground	w: 0.60 m N	0.4	493.4	4,805	4.4
Ridgetop road junction above Shake Canyon	R	2.8	496.2	5,296	1.9
Ridge nose to a junction with a spur trail to Sawmill Campground		2.0	498.2	5,000	-1.6
Road crossing	R	1.2	499.4	4,792	-1.9
Atmore Meadows Spur Road 7N19	R	0.7	500.1	4,705	-1.3
Up to a grassy saddle		2.3	502.4	5,616	4.3
Spur trail to waterless Bear Campground		2.0	504.4	5,400	-1.2
Water Alert (↑): 17.5 m					
Liebre Mountain Truck Trail 7N23	w	0.2	504.6	5,554	8.4
North-descending dirt road	R	0.9	505.5	5,580	0.3
Jeep road	R	1.0	506.5	5,754	1.9
Dirt road	R	0.1	506.6	5,720	-3.7
Jeep track ends		1.0	507.6	5,140	-6.3

SOUTHERN CALIFORNIA

Landmark	Facilities	Diff	S→N	Elev	Gra
Horse Camp		0.5	508.1	4,858	-6.1
Levels out at a dirt road spur	R	1.9	510.0	4,003	-4.9
Small sag pond	w	0.7	510.7	3,800	-3.1
Pine Canyon Road	w, R	0.2	510.9	3,839	2.1
Water Alert (↓): 24.0 m					
Cross a jeep road	R	3.8	514.7	3,522	-0.9
Over-engineered switchbacks to merge with a good jeep road	R	2.1	516.8	3,175	-1.8
CA 138	R	0.8	517.6	3,052	-1.7
269th Street	R	0.5	518.1	2,997	-0.9
Pavement ends		0.4	518.5	2,979	-0.5
Pair of roads that bridge the aqueduct at a siphon	R	1.0	519.5	2,980	0.0
Los Angeles Aqueduct, turning east		0.2	519.7	2,965	-0.8
Faucet east of aqueduct (unreliable)		1.2	520.9	2,889	-0.7
Straight-north course turns east		2.0	522.9	3,090	1.1
Intersection with a good dirt road after Little Oak Canyon Creek	R	6.4	529.3	3,109	0.0
Ignore dirt road, continue on better road	R	3.0	532.3	2,895	-0.8
Triangular junction		0.4	532.7	2,915	0.5
Los Angeles Aqueduct, underground		0.6	533.3	3,105	3.4
Water Alert (↑): 24.0 m					
Cottonwood Creek bridge, check opening on aqueduct for water access	w	1.6	534.9	3,086	-0.1
Water Alert (↓): 23.3 m					
Next dirt road	R	0.1	535.0	3,120	3.7
Resumption of PCT tread		0.4	535.4	3,160	1.1
Bike path overlooking Cottonwood Creek		0.5	535.9	3,250	2.0
East–west jeep road	R	1.0	536.9	3,465	2.3

Landmark	Facilities	Diff	S→N	Elev	Gra
Avangrid Renewables Attn: (Your Name) PCT Hiker 17890 Champagne Ave. Rosamond, CA 93560 661-256-2220, ext. 4321 (call to confirm) Via UPS or FedEx only!	w, R: 1.30 m E	0.0	536.9	3,465	2.3
T-junction, poor dirt roads	R	0.5	537.4	3,609	3.1
Up to a scenic and breezy knoll		0.4	537.8	3,800	5.2
Poor jeep road that traces the south boundary of a barbed wire fence	R	0.2	538.0	3,790	-0.5
Join a good jeep road	R	0.7	538.7	4,070	4.3
End of the fence		0.3	539.0	4,120	1.8
Rough jeep/dirt bike path, west of Tylerhorse Canyon		2.2	541.2	4,960	4.1
Tylerhorse Canyon		0.4	541.6	4,843	-3.2
Saddle overlooking Gamble Spring Canyon		2.9	544.5	4,960	0.4
Gamble Spring Canyon		0.6	545.1	4,643	-5.7
Cross a jeep road	R	3.1	548.2	6,070	5.0
Headwaters of Burham and Pitney Canyons		2.8	551.0	5,980	-0.3
Water Alert (↑):	23.3 m				
Cross Oak Creek via a steel bridge	w	7.2	558.2	4,070	-2.9
Water Alert (↓):	25.1 m				
Paved Tehachapi Willow Springs Road	R	0.3	558.5	4,145	2.7
General Delivery Tehachapi, CA 93581 661-822-0279	PO, w, G, M, L, r, R: 9.40 m W	0.0	558.5	4,145	2.7
General Delivery Mojave, CA 93502 661-824-3502	PO, w, G, M, L, r, R: 12.00 m E	0.0	558.5	4,145	2.7
One good dirt road with plastic marker-posts	R	0.7	559.2	4,165	0.2
Second dirt road	R	0.2	559.4	4,160	-0.3
Up to a small saddle		0.5	559.9	4,495	7.3
Scenic ridgetop		0.5	560.4	4,560	1.4

Landmark	Facilities	Diff	S→N	Elev	Gra
Fourth, good dirt road	R	1.6	562.0	4,485	-0.5
Down to a saddle with a poor dirt road	R	0.5	562.5	4,600	2.5
Cross a dirt road	R	0.6	563.1	4,769	3.1
Cameron Road	R	2.1	565.2	3,900	-4.5
Railroad tracks		0.5	565.7	3,824	-1.6
Tehachapi Pass (CA 58), start of Sierra Nevada	R	0.7	566.4	3,825	0.0
Gate opposite the CAMERON ROAD EXIT 1 MILE sign	R	1.3	567.7	3,781	-0.4
Colorful view of Waterfall Canyon	R	5.2	572.9	6,055	4.8
Head of Waterfall Canyon		1.8	574.7	6,115	0.4
Seldom-used jeep road		0.4	575.1	6,126	0.3
0.2 mile from the gated road, after the SKY RIVER RANCH sign	R	4.4	579.5	6,005	-0.3
Water Alert (↑): 25.1 m					
Golden Oaks Spring	w	3.8	583.3	5,474	-1.5
Water Alert (↓): 18.8 m					
Cross a green gate in a cattle fence		6.7	590.0	5,103	-0.6
Large grassy area	R	2.9	592.9	5,018	-0.3
East–west road	R	0.1	593.0	5,009	-1.0
Hamp Williams Pass		3.5	596.5	5,521	1.6
Curve of a private dirt road	R	3.2	599.7	5,620	0.3
T-junction		0.8	600.5	5,996	5.1
Ascend along a tight right curve, PCT path on left		0.4	600.9	6,160	4.5
Water Alert (↑): 18.7 m					
Cross a dirt road leading to Robin Bird Spring	w, R: 0.10 m W	1.1	602.0	6,329	1.7
Jawbone Canyon Road	R	0.5	602.5	6,609	6.1
Log footbridge over branch of Cottonwood Creek	w	1.5	604.0	6,467	-1.0

SOUTHERN CALIFORNIA

Landmark	Facilities	Diff	S→N	Elev	Gra
Logging road	R	1.0	605.0	6,720	2.7
Cement structure	R	0.7	605.7	6,750	0.5
Landers Creek	w: 0.20 m W	1.4	607.1	6,337	-3.2
Piute Mountain Road	R	1.0	608.1	6,211	-1.4
Sequoia National Forest Road 29S05	w, R: 0.30 m N	0.8	608.9	6,313	1.4
Water Alert (↓): 35.1 m					
Piute Mountain Road again, summit of Harris Grade	R	2.3	611.2	6,611	1.4
Kelso Valley Road at a pass	R	4.8	616.0	4,954	-3.7
Butterbredt Canyon Road, Kelso Valley Road to a spring	w, R: 1.20 m N	1.8	617.8	4,551	-2.4
First junction to Willow Spring	w, R: 1.60 m N	2.2	620.0	4,533	-0.1
Slopes of Pinyon Mountain, multi-road-and-path junction to Willow Spring	w, R: 1.60 m NW	1.9	621.9	5,285	4.3
Another multi-road-and-trail junction	R	1.7	623.6	5,385	0.6
A ridgecrest saddle		1.1	624.7	5,700	3.1
SC 328 road on a crest-line saddle	R	0.7	625.4	5,296	-6.3
SC 47 road on another crest-line saddle	R	0.1	625.5	5,286	-1.1
SC 37 road	R	2.9	628.4	5,731	1.7
Junction at Bird Spring Pass		2.5	630.9	5,355	-1.6
Ridge with a westward orientation		2.4	633.3	6,460	5.0
Highest point before Walker Pass and beyond		1.3	634.6	6,940	4.0
Road to Yellow Jacket Spring	w, R: 0.70 m NW	2.4	637.0	6,257	-3.1
Join the road to McIvers Spring	R	4.5	641.5	6,681	1.0
Water Alert (↑): 35.2 m					
Junction to McIvers Spring	w: 0.20 m E	2.3	643.8	6,692	0.1
Curve around a sharp canyon crease		3.0	646.8	6,680	0.0
Ridgeline saddle after Jacks Creek		2.2	649.0	5,860	-4.0

SOUTHERN CALIFORNIA

Landmark	Facilities	Diff	S→N	Elev	Gra
Path leading to Walker Pass Trailhead Campground	w: 0.10 m N	2.3	651.3	5,068	-3.7
Water Alert (↓): 12.8 m					
Historical marker		0.7	652.0	5,264	3.0
General Delivery Onyx, CA 93255 760-378-2121	PO, w, G, r, R: 17.60 m W	0.0	652.0	5,264	3.0
North-facing slopes to a saddle		4.1	656.1	6,585	3.5
Morris–Jenkins saddle		0.8	656.9	6,509	-1.0
Commemorative plaque		0.2	657.1	6,605	5.2
Rounded point of a ridge		1.4	658.5	6,950	2.7
Jenkins–Owens saddle		2.3	660.8	7,020	0.3
A lesser saddle		1.4	662.2	6,300	-5.6
Rough dirt road	R	1.2	663.4	5,500	-7.3
Water Alert (↑): 12.6 m					
Joshua Tree Spring	w: 0.25 m SW	0.4	663.8	5,481	-0.5
Cross a ridge at a saddle		1.2	665.0	5,240	-2.2
Northwest to another saddle		1.4	666.4	5,860	4.8
Headwaters branch of Spanish Needle Creek	w	2.3	668.7	5,105	-3.6
Spring-fed branch of Spanish Needle Creek	w	0.7	669.4	5,269	2.5
Spanish Needle Creek (third encounter)	w	0.8	670.2	5,637	5.0
Ridge between Spanish Needle group and Lamont Peak		2.6	672.8	6,761	4.7
Second broader saddle		3.3	676.1	6,899	0.5
Sierra Crest saddle with limited views		1.4	677.5	6,260	-5.0
Seasonal creek		0.8	678.3	5,950	-4.2
Chimney Creek	w, R: 0.30 m NE	2.5	680.8	5,539	-1.8
Canebrake Road	w, R: 0.30 m NE	0.1	680.9	5,560	2.3
Fox Mill Spring	w	2.2	683.1	6,517	4.7

Landmark	Facilities	Diff	S→N	Elev	Gra
Dirt road	R	0.1	683.2	6,581	7.0
Trail summit		4.0	687.2	8,020	3.9
Road crossing	R	0.2	687.4	7,980	-2.2
Chimney Basin Road	R	1.7	689.1	7,226	-4.8
Spur ridge before Rockhouse Basin		2.5	691.6	6,600	-2.7
Manter Creek in Rockhouse Basin	w	1.9	693.5	5,846	-4.3
South Fork Kern River	w	4.4	697.9	5,750	-1.2
Stream	w	2.0	699.9	5,933	1.0
Closed off-highway vehicle road	R	0.6	700.5	5,980	0.9
Bridge near Kennedy Meadows General Store		1.7	702.2	6,009	0.2
Kennedy Meadows General Store Attn: (Your Name) PCT Hiker 96740 Beach Meadow Road Inyokern, CA 93527 559-850-5647 $6 fee	w, G, r, R: 0.70 m SE	0.0	702.2	6,009	0.2

PACIFIC CREST TRAIL: Central California

Belden Town Resort
1,286.9 mi.

Meadow Valley
1,267.9 mi.

Sierra City
1,195.4 mi.

Soda Springs,
Donner Ski Ranch,
and Truckee 1,153.4 mi.

Tahoe City
1,124.8 mi.

Olympic 1,139.4 mi.

Carson City

Meyers Post Office
1,091.0 mi.

South Lake Tahoe
1,090.8 mi.

Kennedy Meadows
Resort 1,016.9 mi.

Tuolumne
Meadows
942.5 mi.

Mammoth Lakes
903.0 mi.

Vermilion Valley
Resort 878.7 mi.

Bishop 831.0 mi.

Mono Hot Springs 872.4 mi.

Muir
Trail Ranch
857.7 mi.

Independence
788.9 mi.

Lone Pine
745.3 mi.

Kennedy
Meadows
702.2 mi.

Honey
Lake

PLUMAS
NATIONAL
FOREST

Pyramid
Lake

Reno

TAHOE
NATIONAL
FOREST

Yuba City

ELDORADO
NATIONAL
FOREST

Lake
Tahoe

HUMBOLDT-
TOIYABE
NATIONAL
FOREST

Sacramento

NEVADA
CALIFORNIA

STANISLAUS
NATIONAL
FOREST

San Francisco

Modesto

YOSEMITE
NATIONAL
PARK

San Jose

SIERRA
NATIONAL
FOREST

INYO
NATIONAL
FOREST

Fresno

SEQUOIA
AND KINGS
CANYON
NATIONAL
PARK

20 miles

20 kilometers

CENTRAL CALIFORNIA

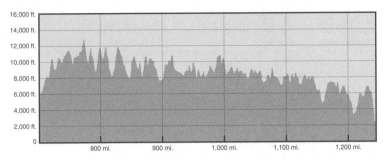

**Elevation Profile for Central California
From Kennedy Meadows to Belden**

SEGMENT TOTAL MILEAGE: 584.1 MILES

Landmark	Facilities	Diff	S→N	Elev	Gra
Cross a road	R	1.8	704.0	6,080	0.4
Cross the road again	R	0.4	704.4	6,120	1.1
Kennedy Meadows Campground	w	0.3	704.7	6,146	0.9
Junction leaving Clover Meadow Trail		1.1	705.8	6,240	0.9
Steel-girder wooden bridge	w	0.8	706.6	6,288	0.7
Crag Creek	w	2.0	708.6	6,815	2.9
Old Clover Meadow Trail		2.5	711.1	7,560	3.2
T-junction with Haiwee Trail 37E01		1.2	712.3	8,070	4.6
Beck Meadows Trail 35E15		1.1	713.4	7,939	-1.3
Deer Mountain's northern ridge		2.2	715.6	8,390	2.2
South Fork Kern River bridge in Monache Meadows	w	0.9	716.5	7,832	-6.7
Southeast-heading trail to Kennedy Meadows		0.1	716.6	7,840	0.9
Right turn at a junction		0.1	716.7	7,840	0.0
Low ridge		1.2	717.9	8,050	1.9
Cow Creek	w	1.3	719.2	8,321	2.3

43

Landmark	Facilities	Diff	S→N	Elev	Gra
Olancha Pass Trail		1.4	720.6	9,106	6.1
Trail junction after Cow Creek		0.1	720.7	9,189	9.0
North to a lateral trail		0.2	720.9	9,240	2.8
After Monache Creek bowl, path levels off on a saddle west of Olancha Peak		3.5	724.4	10,580	4.2
Cross a year-round creek	w	3.7	728.1	9,045	-4.5
Meadow-side causeway trail at Gomez Meadow		0.9	729.0	8,987	-0.7
Step-across year-round Death Canyon Creek	w	1.8	730.8	8,951	-0.2
Crest-line saddle		3.7	734.5	10,390	4.2
Junction with a faint 0.5-mile-long lateral trail to a spring	w: 0.30 m N	1.9	736.4	10,364	-0.1
Second saddle with path signed CORRAL		1.6	738.0	10,260	-0.7
Descent northwest to an obscure path		1.8	739.8	10,000	-1.6
Sierra Crest at a low saddle to Diaz Creek	w: 0.50 m E	1.9	741.7	9,672	-1.9
CORRAL junction sign	w: 0.20 m N	1.3	743.0	9,952	2.3
Mulkey Pass		1.5	744.5	10,394	3.2
Trail Pass Trail		0.8	745.3	10,492	1.3
General Delivery Lone Pine, CA 93545 760-876-5681	PO, w, G, M, L, r, R: 24.90 m E	0.0	745.3	10,492	1.3
Path to Poison Meadow		1.3	746.6	10,740	2.1
Intersect the crest at a saddle		0.6	747.2	10,740	0.0
Cottonwood Pass		3.0	750.2	11,132	1.4
Chicken Spring Lake outlet	w	0.6	750.8	11,213	1.5
Seasonal creek	w	2.5	753.3	11,349	0.6
Sequoia National Park border		0.6	753.9	11,361	0.2
Siberian Pass/Rock Creek Trail		0.9	754.8	11,083	-3.4
Down to a junction with Rock Creek Trail		4.5	759.3	9,940	-2.8
Cross a brook	w	0.3	759.6	9,840	-3.6

Landmark	Facilities	Diff	S→N	Elev	Gra
Rock Creek crossing	w	0.9	760.5	9,518	-3.9
Guyot Creek	w	1.3	761.8	10,363	7.1
Pass northeast of 12,300' Mount Guyot		1.0	762.8	10,920	6.1
Crabtree Meadow with lateral trail to Mount Whitney	w	3.5	766.3	10,321	-1.9
Path north-northwest to a signed junction with John Muir Trail (JMT) to Mount Whitney		0.7	767.0	10,779	7.1
Saddle above Sandy Meadow		1.7	768.7	10,964	1.2
Wallace Creek and High Sierra Trail junction	w	1.6	770.3	10,392	-3.9
Ford Wright Creek	w	0.7	771.0	10,700	4.8
Tyndall Frog Ponds	w	3.1	774.1	11,042	1.2
Shepherd Pass Trail	w	0.5	774.6	10,923	-2.6
Ford Tyndall Creek		0.1	774.7	10,977	5.9
Lake South America Trail		0.2	774.9	11,049	3.9
Forester Pass		4.6	779.5	13,118	4.9
Center Basin Trail	w	4.8	784.3	10,480	-6.0
Upper Vidette Meadow	w	1.8	786.1	9,912	-3.4
Vidette Meadow	w	0.9	787.0	9,554	-4.3
Junction up Bubbs Creek canyon		0.3	787.3	9,562	0.3
Bullfrog Lake junction		1.2	788.5	10,525	8.7
Kearsarge Pass Trail junction for north-bound hikers		0.4	788.9	10,746	6.0
General Delivery Independence, CA 93526 760-878-2210	PO, w, G, M, L, r, R: 24.00 m E	0.0	788.9	10,746	6.0
Kearsarge Pass Trail junction for south-bound hikers		0.2	789.1	10,775	1.6
Glen Pass		2.0	791.1	11,946	6.4
Sixty Lakes Basin Trail junction	w	1.8	792.9	10,563	-8.4
Dragon Lake Trail junction		0.4	793.3	10,560	-0.1
Rae Lakes Ranger Station junction		0.6	793.9	10,604	0.8

CENTRAL CALIFORNIA

Landmark	Facilities	Diff	S→N	Elev	Gra
Arrowhead Lake	w	1.3	795.2	10,315	-2.1
Dollar Lake (unsigned Baxter Pass Trail)	w	0.7	795.9	10,217	-2.3
Woods Creek	w	3.9	799.8	8,532	-4.7
Sawmill Pass Trail	w	3.6	803.4	10,369	5.5
Pinchot Pass		3.7	807.1	12,142	5.2
Lake Marjorie outlet	w	1.8	808.9	11,137	-6.1
Bench Lake Trail	w	1.2	810.1	10,770	-3.3
Taboose Pass Trail	w	0.1	810.2	10,778	0.9
South Fork Kings River Trail	w	1.2	811.4	10,039	-6.7
South Fork Kings River ford	w	2.3	813.7	10,835	3.8
Mather Pass		3.2	816.9	12,097	4.3
Upper Palisade Lake	w	2.4	819.3	10,842	-5.7
Lower Palisade Lake	w	1.0	820.3	10,600	-2.6
Deer Meadow	w	3.1	823.4	8,892	-6.0
Middle Fork Kings River	w	4.0	827.4	8,038	-2.3
Bishop Pass Trail	w	3.6	831.0	8,751	2.1
General Delivery Bishop, CA 93514 760-873-3526	PO, w, G, M, L, r, R: 33.30 m NE	0.0	831.0	8,751	2.1
Helen Lake	w	6.4	837.4	11,631	4.9
Muir Pass		1.2	838.6	11,974	3.1
Evolution Creek	w	2.2	840.8	11,372	-3.0
Evolution Lake Inlet	w	2.4	843.2	10,850	-2.4
McClure Meadow	w	5.0	848.2	9,652	-2.6
Evolution Creek crossing	w	2.7	850.9	9,201	-1.8
South Fork San Joaquin River footbridge	w	1.5	852.4	8,482	-5.2
Piute Pass Trail	w	3.5	855.9	8,072	-1.3
Florence Lake Trail		1.8	857.7	7,889	-1.1

CENTRAL CALIFORNIA

Landmark	Facilities	Diff	S→N	Elev	Gra
Muir Trail Ranch Attn: (Your Name) PCT Hiker PO Box 176 Lakeshore, CA 93634; muirtrailranch.com	w: 1.50 m NW;R	0.0	857.7	7,889	-1.1
Florence Lake and Sallie Keyes Cutoff Trails		1.8	859.5	8,411	3.1
Senger Creek	w	2.1	861.6	9,748	6.9
Unmaintained trail to South Fork of San Joaquin River		1.7	863.3	10,140	2.5
Sallie Keyes Lakes	w	0.4	863.7	10,200	1.6
Heart Lake	w	0.8	864.5	10,550	4.8
Selden Pass		1.1	865.6	10,910	3.6
Marie Lake outlet	w	0.9	866.5	10,570	-4.1
Rosemarie Meadow		1.4	867.9	10,037	-4.1
Seven Gables Lake Trail junction up East Fork Bear Creek	w	1.3	869.2	9,578	-3.8
Lake Italy Trail	w	1.2	870.4	9,328	-2.3
Bear Creek Trail to Mono Hot Springs	w	2.0	872.4	8,944	-2.1
Bear Ridge Trail	w	2.1	874.5	9,874	4.8
Mono Creek	w	4.2	878.7	7,877	-5.2
Vermilion Valley Resort c/o China Peak Landing Attn: (Your Name) PCT Hiker 62311 Huntington Lake Road Lakeshore, CA 93634 559-259-4000; edisonlake.com Via UPS or FedEx only!	w, G, M, L, R: 6.00 m W	0.0	878.7	7,877	-5.2
Mono Pass Trail		1.4	880.1	8,356	3.7
North Fork Mono Creek	w	1.4	881.5	8,993	4.9
Re-ford North Fork Mono Creek	w	1.2	882.7	9,640	5.9
Silver Pass		2.2	884.9	10,747	5.5
Goodale Pass Trail	w	1.1	886.0	10,538	-2.1
Cascade Valley Trail (alternate route)	w	2.5	888.5	9,204	-5.8

Landmark	Facilities	Diff	S→N	Elev	Gra
Tully Hole	w	1.0	889.5	9,524	3.5
Lake Virginia	w	2.1	891.6	10,350	4.3
Purple Lake	w	1.9	893.5	9,917	-2.5
Trail to Duck Lake	w	2.2	895.7	10,174	1.3
Deer Creek	w	5.3	901.0	9,115	-2.2
Upper Crater Meadow		2.0	903.0	8,931	-1.0
General Delivery Mammoth Lakes, CA 93546 760-934-2205	PO, w, G, M, L, r, R: 7.25 m NE	0.0	903.0	8,931	-1.0
Trail to Horseshoe Lake	w	0.9	903.9	8,660	-3.3
Boundary Creek	w	1.8	905.7	8,039	-3.7
Abandoned stagecoach road	R	0.9	906.6	7,718	-3.9
Red's Meadow, few supplies	w, G, M, L: 0.30 m N	0.0	906.6	7,718	-3.9
Red's Meadow, Rainbow Falls–Fish Valley–Cascade Valley Trail (end of alternate route)		0.2	906.8	7,629	-4.8
Trail junction by east boundary of Devils Postpile National Monument (alternate route)		0.4	907.2	7,480	-4.0
Summit Meadow Trail		1.1	908.3	7,710	2.3
JMT and PCT diverge (alternate routes)		0.7	909.0	7,681	-0.4
Minaret Creek	w	0.6	909.6	7,617	-1.2
Bridge across Middle Fork San Joaquin River		1.4	911.0	7,680	0.5
Permanent stream along Middle Fork	w	1.0	912.0	7,810	1.4
Another stream	w	1.1	913.1	7,910	1.0
Junction after a small knoll		0.5	913.6	8,078	3.6
River Trail		0.5	914.1	8,285	4.5
Agnew Meadows Road	w, R	0.7	914.8	8,311	0.4
Views of Ritter Range		3.2	918.0	9,680	4.6
Junction with trail over Agnew Pass		2.4	920.4	9,735	0.2

CENTRAL CALIFORNIA

Landmark	Facilities	Diff	S→N	Elev	Gra
Middle Fork–Clark Lakes Trail		0.6	921.0	9,507	-4.1
De facto trail, pass a lakelet	w	0.3	921.3	9,590	3.0
River Trail		0.6	921.9	9,610	0.4
Thousand Island Lake (end of alternate route)	w	1.0	922.9	9,846	2.6
Island Pass		1.7	924.6	10,227	2.4
Obscure junction to Davis Lake		1.0	925.6	9,699	-5.7
Rush Creek Trail	w	0.3	925.9	9,645	-2.0
Marie Lakes Trail		1.0	926.9	10,062	4.5
Donohue Pass		2.6	929.5	11,073	4.2
Lyell Fork crossing	w	1.7	931.2	10,186	-5.7
Another Lyell Fork crossing	w	0.9	932.1	9,651	-6.5
Junction to Vogelsang High Sierra Camp	w	4.0	936.1	8,888	-2.1
Vogelsang Trail		4.1	940.2	8,722	-0.4
Junction to Tuolumne Meadows Campground		0.6	940.8	8,669	-1.0
Dana Fork of the Tuolumne River	w	0.7	941.5	8,688	0.3
Tuolumne Meadows Lodge's road	R	0.2	941.7	8,671	-0.9
CA 120	R	0.8	942.5	8,596	-1.0
General Delivery Tuolumne Meadows, CA 95389 209-372-4475	PO, w, G: 0.30 m SW; L: 1.30 m E; r: 0.30 m W; R	0.0	942.5	8,596	-1.0
Fork just beyond a minor gap		0.7	943.2	8,596	0.0
Soda Springs area		0.1	943.3	8,600	0.4
Delaney Creek	w	0.8	944.1	8,612	0.2
Young Lakes Trail		0.4	944.5	8,650	1.0
Bridge over Tuolumne River	w	2.5	947.0	8,303	-1.5
Junction to McGee Lake		1.1	948.1	7,975	-3.2
Glen Aulin, next to Conness Creek	w	0.2	948.3	7,890	-4.6

CENTRAL CALIFORNIA

Landmark	Facilities	Diff	S→N	Elev	Gra
Forested gap along Cold Canyon Creek		2.9	951.2	8,768	3.3
McCabe Lakes Trail		3.9	955.1	9,106	0.9
McCabe Creek		0.9	956.0	8,531	-6.9
Virginia Canyon Trail	w	0.2	956.2	8,533	0.1
Forested pass		2.2	958.4	9,560	5.1
Miller Lake	w	1.4	959.8	9,467	-0.7
Low gap		0.6	960.4	9,598	2.4
Matterhorn Canyon Trail	w	1.6	962.0	8,499	-7.5
Wilson Creek, last ford	w	3.3	965.3	9,473	3.2
Benson Pass		1.1	966.4	10,125	6.4
South shore of Smedberg Lake	w	2.0	968.4	9,219	-4.9
Well-defined gap		0.3	968.7	9,340	4.4
Junction to Rodgers and Neall Lakes		0.8	969.5	9,461	1.6
Junction to Murdock Lake		0.3	969.8	9,390	-2.6
First ford of Smedberg Lake's outlet	w	0.7	970.5	8,735	-10.0
Second ford of Smedberg Lake's outlet	w	1.0	971.5	8,247	-5.3
Benson Lake Trail junction		1.2	972.7	7,601	-5.9
Wind-free, sparkling pond	w	2.1	974.8	9,002	7.3
Seavey Pass	w	0.8	975.6	9,091	1.2
Highest gap		0.2	975.8	9,180	4.8
Junction in Kerrick Canyon		0.4	976.2	8,820	-9.8
Bear Valley–Yosemite Valley–Pleasant Valley Trail junction	w	3.5	979.7	7,978	-2.6
Rancheria Creek	w	0.1	979.8	7,973	-0.5
North to a shallow gap		1.3	981.1	8,700	6.1
Stubblefield Canyon Creek	w	1.3	982.4	7,752	-7.9
Macomb Ridge pass		2.1	984.5	8,910	6.0
Tilden Lake Trail signed junction	w	1.1	985.6	8,384	-5.2

CENTRAL CALIFORNIA

Landmark	Facilities	Diff	S→N	Elev	Gra
Wilma (or Wilmer) Lake	w	1.3	986.9	7,958	-3.6
Junction with Laurel Lake Trail to Jack Main Canyon	w	0.5	987.4	7,959	0.0
Junction east to Tilden Lake	w	1.7	989.1	8,172	1.4
South end of Grace Meadow		3.7	992.8	8,653	1.4
First trail to Bond Pass		2.9	995.7	9,360	2.6
Dorothy Lake Pass		1.4	997.1	9,552	1.5
Lake Harriet	w	1.2	998.3	9,245	-2.8
Cascade Creek footbridge	w	0.7	999.0	9,040	-3.2
Junction to West Walker River Trail	w	0.5	999.5	9,040	0.0
Junction with Cinko Lake Trail just past a creek after three ponds	w	0.8	1,000.3	8,925	-1.6
West Fork West Walker River Trail	w	1.9	1,002.2	8,675	-1.4
West Fork West Walker River bridge, junction by Lower Long Lake	w	0.2	1,002.4	8,590	-4.6
Another creek	w	1.5	1,003.9	8,552	-0.3
Kennedy Canyon Creek	w	2.0	1,005.9	9,063	2.8
Emigrant Pass Trail junction	R	1.2	1,007.1	9,713	5.9
Leave jeep road at a switchback (alternate route)	R	1.8	1,008.9	10,583	5.3
Sierra Crest		2.3	1,011.2	10,640	0.3
Ridge, highest point after Donohue Pass		0.8	1,012.0	10,898	3.5
Notch on a steep wall		0.7	1,012.7	10,805	-1.4
Another crest crossing		0.8	1,013.5	10,760	-0.6
Another crest crossing		1.1	1,014.6	10,870	1.1
First creek since Kennedy Canyon	w	1.7	1,016.3	9,839	-6.6
Sonora Pass (CA 108) (end of alternate route)	R	0.6	1,016.9	9,655	-3.3
Kennedy Meadows Resort and Pack Station Attn: (Your Name) PCT Hiker 42421 CA 108 Pinecrest, CA 95364 Via UPS only! kennedymeadows.com for details	w, G, M, L, sh, r, R: 10.20 m W	0.0	1,016.9	9,655	-3.3

CENTRAL CALIFORNIA

Landmark	Facilities	Diff	S→N	Elev	Gra
Trailhead-parking spur		0.2	1,017.1	9,610	-2.4
Start switchback		1.6	1,018.7	10,146	3.6
County-line ridge		0.7	1,019.4	10,403	4.0
Top the Sierra Crest at a saddle		0.4	1,019.8	10,527	3.4
Junction atop Wolf Creek Lake saddle to Wolf Creek Lake	w: 0.33 m S	1.2	1,021.0	10,259	-2.4
East Carson River Trail, descend to a small flat	w	5.2	1,026.2	8,128	-4.5
Prominent crest saddle, junction to Boulder Lake		3.0	1,029.2	8,576	1.6
Boulder Creek	w	1.5	1,030.7	8,655	0.6
Descend to a saddle by Golden Lake		2.3	1,033.0	9,184	2.5
Junction with Paradise Valley and Golden Canyon Trails		1.3	1,034.3	9,194	0.1
Saddle with view of Peak 9,501		0.7	1,035.0	9,323	2.0
Another saddle after Murray Canyon		1.4	1,036.4	9,070	-2.0
East Fork of Wolf Creek	w	1.9	1,038.3	8,329	-4.2
Middle Fork of Wolf Creek	w	0.5	1,038.8	8,304	-0.5
Multibranched West Fork of Wolf Creek	w	0.4	1,039.2	8,404	2.7
Sierra Crest		0.7	1,039.9	8,717	4.9
Wolf Creek Pass	w	1.0	1,040.9	8,414	-3.3
Junction by a gully to Asa Lake		0.2	1,041.1	8,507	5.1
Asa Lake's outlet creek	w	0.2	1,041.3	8,523	0.9
Bull Canyon Trail		2.3	1,043.6	9,112	2.8
Noble Lake	w	0.4	1,044.0	8,959	-4.2
Noble Lake's outlet creek	w	0.2	1,044.2	8,900	-3.2
Junction with northern part of Noble Canyon Trail	w	1.1	1,045.3	8,400	-4.9
Ebbetts Pass Trail	R	2.8	1,048.1	8,743	1.3
CA 4 near Ebbetts Pass	R	0.3	1,048.4	8,702	-1.5

Landmark	Facilities	Diff	S→N	Elev	Gra
Sherrold Lake	w	0.5	1,048.9	8,769	1.5
Raymond Meadows Creek	w	3.1	1,052.0	8,658	-0.4
Eagle Creek	w	1.1	1,053.1	8,352	-3.0
Deep crest saddle		1.3	1,054.4	8,510	1.3
Pennsylvania Creek	w	0.6	1,055.0	8,140	-6.7
Sagebrush saddle		1.0	1,056.0	8,660	5.7
Side trail to Raymond Lake		1.6	1,057.6	8,653	0.0
Raymond Lake creek	w	1.0	1,058.6	8,116	-5.8
Conspicuous saddle		0.8	1,059.4	8,230	1.5
Pleasant Valley Trail 008		0.6	1,060.0	7,820	-7.4
Tributary of Pleasant Valley Creek	w	0.5	1,060.5	7,871	1.1
Saddle leaving the eastern part of Mokelumne Wilderness		0.5	1,061.0	8,084	4.6
Spur trail to Wet Meadows Trailhead		0.1	1,061.1	8,160	8.3
Reach a road	R	1.3	1,062.4	7,879	-2.3
Lily Pad Lake	w	0.6	1,063.0	7,861	-0.3
Outlet creek of Tamarack Lake	w	1.4	1,064.4	7,843	-0.1
Spur trail to PCT parking lot		0.8	1,065.2	8,003	2.2
Blue Lakes Road	R	0.3	1,065.5	8,136	4.8
Saddle southeast of The Nipple		2.4	1,067.9	8,834	3.2
Lost Lakes spur road	w: 0.10 m NE; R	1.8	1,069.7	8,659	-1.1
Muddy pond		1.6	1,071.3	8,834	1.2
Summit City Canyon Trail 18E07		0.2	1,071.5	8,910	4.1
Forestdale Creek	w	0.9	1,072.4	8,608	-3.6
Junction to Winnemucca Lake		2.9	1,075.3	8,899	1.1
Frog Lake	w	0.1	1,075.4	8,870	-3.1
CA 88, south end of a long parking lot with Carson Pass markers	R	1.3	1,076.7	8,590	-2.3

Landmark	Facilities	Diff	S→N	Elev	Gra
Flat parking area		0.1	1,076.8	8,561	-3.1
Pond-blessed saddle	w	1.3	1,078.1	8,764	1.7
Upper Truckee River	w	1.3	1,079.4	8,390	-3.1
Branch right after two cabins		0.3	1,079.7	8,379	-0.4
Ford of Upper Truckee River	w	0.6	1,080.3	8,330	-0.9
Second trail from Schneider Camp		1.5	1,081.8	8,698	2.7
Showers Lake	w	0.1	1,081.9	8,654	-4.8
Showers Lake outlet	w	0.1	1,082.0	8,587	-7.3
Trail 17E16		1.8	1,083.8	8,970	2.3
Shallow gap		0.2	1,084.0	8,890	-4.3
Junction with Sayles Canyon Trail 17E14		1.2	1,085.2	8,630	-2.4
Bryan Meadow		0.8	1,086.0	8,517	-1.5
Second creek crossing by Benwood Meadow	w	1.3	1,087.3	8,341	-1.5
Benwood Meadow's north edge		1.7	1,089.0	7,520	-5.2
Road to Echo Summit parking lot	R	1.0	1,090.0	7,388	-1.4
US 50	R	0.8	1,090.8	7,241	-2.0
General Delivery South Lake Tahoe, CA 96150 530-544-5867	PO, w, G, M, L, sh, R: 9.70 m NE	0.0	1,090.8	7,241	-2.0
Johnson Pass Road		0.2	1,091.0	7,321	4.3
General Delivery, Meyers Post Office 1285 Apache Ave. South Lake Tahoe, CA 96150 530-577-5081	PO, w, G, M, R: 3.55 m NE	0.0	1,091.0	7,321	4.3
Echo Chalet	w, G	1.2	1,092.2	7,497	1.6
Lower Echo Lake	w	0.1	1,092.3	7,427	-7.6
Junction to water taxi		2.6	1,094.9	7,474	0.2
Junction to a saddle and Triangle Lake		0.6	1,095.5	7,715	4.4
Another trail junction		0.5	1,096.0	7,865	3.3

CENTRAL CALIFORNIA

Landmark	Facilities	Diff	S→N	Elev	Gra
Lateral trail above Triangle Lake		0.6	1,096.6	8,226	6.5
Junction to Lake of the Woods		0.4	1,097.0	8,318	2.5
Past a trail to Lake Aloha, above Lake Margery		0.6	1,097.6	8,331	0.2
Past a trail going to Lake Margery		0.2	1,097.8	8,299	-1.7
Junction above Lake Aloha		0.6	1,098.4	8,134	-3.0
Reach a gully	w	0.5	1,098.9	8,193	1.3
Rubicon Trail (alternate route)		1.0	1,099.9	8,128	-0.7
Heather Lake's northwest shore	w	0.6	1,100.5	7,906	-4.0
Cross Susie Lake's outlet creek	w	1.1	1,101.6	7,776	-1.3
Swampy meadow where the trail forks to the Fallen Leaf area	w, G, R: 4.50 m E	0.6	1,102.2	7,682	-1.7
Another intersection to the Fallen Leaf area	w, G: 4.30 m E	0.4	1,102.6	7,920	6.5
Trail 17E09 to Gilmore Lake	w: 0.25 m NE	0.6	1,103.2	8,288	6.7
Dicks Pass		2.5	1,105.7	9,377	4.7
Descend to a rocky saddle, reach a junction to Eagle Falls Picnic Area		1.7	1,107.4	8,489	-5.7
Reach a spur trail to Dicks Lake		0.2	1,107.6	8,420	-3.7
Fontanillis Lake		1.0	1,108.6	8,288	-1.4
Trail junction above Middle Velma Lake		0.9	1,109.5	7,972	-3.8
Trail descending west to Camper Flat (end of alternate route)		0.3	1,109.8	7,927	-1.6
Junction to Phipps Pass		1.2	1,111.0	8,092	1.5
Seasonal Phipps Creek	w	1.6	1,112.6	7,630	-3.1
High point, almost to Peak 8,235		2.0	1,114.6	8,105	2.6
Junction to General Creek and Lake Genevieve		0.9	1,115.5	7,869	-2.8
Leave Desolation Wilderness	R	1.7	1,117.2	7,541	-2.1
Jeep road atop a forested saddle	R	1.0	1,118.2	7,570	0.3
Richardson Lake's northwest corner	w	0.4	1,118.6	7,407	-4.4

Central California

CENTRAL CALIFORNIA

Landmark	Facilities	Diff	S→N	Elev	Gra
Lightly used road by Miller Creek	w, R	1.8	1,120.4	7,021	-2.3
McKinney–Rubicon Springs Road 16E75	R	0.1	1,120.5	7,022	0.1
Bear Lake's outlet creek	w, R	1.6	1,122.1	6,973	-0.3
Blackwood Canyon Road	R	0.4	1,122.5	7,084	3.0
Forest Route 3 near Barker Pass		2.3	1,124.8	7,658	2.7
General Delivery Tahoe City, CA 96145 530-583-4900	PO, w, G, M, L, R: 12.00 m NE	0.0	1,124.8	7,658	2.7
Dirt road		0.9	1,125.7	8,050	4.7
Saddle after a spring-fed gully		0.7	1,126.4	8,262	3.3
North Fork Blackwood Creek	w	0.7	1,127.1	7,954	-4.8
Enter Granite Chief Wilderness, low knoll with excellent views		2.4	1,129.5	8,341	1.8
PCT and Tahoe Rim Trail split		0.2	1,129.7	8,402	3.3
Ward Peak maintenance road	R	3.3	1,133.0	8,379	-0.1
Five Lakes Creek	w	2.9	1,135.9	7,426	-3.6
Whiskey Creek Trail 16E02		1.0	1,136.9	7,110	-3.4
Tevis Cup Trail 16E04		2.2	1,139.1	7,949	4.1
Junction to Emigrant Pass marker		0.3	1,139.4	8,086	5.0
General Delivery Olympic, CA 96146 530-583-5126	PO, w, G, M, L, R: 3.80 m E	0.0	1,139.4	8,086	5.0
Junction to Emigrant Pass		0.7	1,140.1	8,419	5.2
Headwaters of Squaw Creek	w	0.7	1,140.8	8,257	-2.5
Water Alert (↓): 12.9 m					
Granite Chief Trail 15E23 to Squaw Valley		1.1	1,141.9	8,185	-0.7
Painted Rock Trail 15E06		1.5	1,143.4	7,552	-4.6
Flat section below the trail		1.1	1,144.5	7,945	3.9
Tinker Knob saddle, junction with Cold Stream Trail		1.2	1,145.7	8,639	6.3

CENTRAL CALIFORNIA

Landmark	Facilities	Diff	S→N	Elev	Gra
Sierra Crest		0.2	1,145.9	8,745	5.8
Saddle north of Anderson Peak		1.7	1,147.6	8,256	-3.1
Round Peak 8,374 to a shallower saddle		0.5	1,148.1	8,170	-1.9
Weather station		2.4	1,150.5	7,991	-0.8
South end of Mount Judah Loop		0.6	1,151.1	7,879	-2.0
Cross one-lane road	R	0.7	1,151.8	7,520	-5.6
North end of Mount Judah Loop		0.4	1,152.2	7,547	0.7
Road junction to Lake Mary homesites	R	1.0	1,153.2	7,060	-5.3
Water Alert (↑): 12.6 m					
Historic US 40 near Donner Pass	w, G, M, L, sh, R: 0.25 m W	0.2	1,153.4	7,114	2.9
Donner Ski Ranch Attn: (Your Name) PCT Hiker 19320 Donner Pass Road PO Box 66 Norden, CA 95724 530-426-3635; donnerskiranch.com	w, M, L, sh, r, R: 0.25 m W	0.0	1,153.4	7,114	2.9
General Delivery Soda Springs, CA 95728 530-426-3082	PO, w, G, M, r, R: 3.20 m W	0.0	1,153.4	7,114	2.9
General Delivery Truckee, CA 96161 530-587-7158	PO, w, G, M, L, r, R: 12.00 m E	0.0	1,153.4	7,114	2.9
Small pond	w	1.2	1,154.6	7,201	0.8
Shallow saddle		1.4	1,156.0	7,206	0.0
Junction to parking lot, 0.25 mile south of I-80		0.7	1,156.7	7,220	0.2
Tunnels underneath I-80		0.3	1,157.0	7,200	-0.7
Northwest to a road	R	1.6	1,158.6	7,431	1.6
Castle Pass		1.3	1,159.9	7,928	4.2
Peter Grubb Hut		0.9	1,160.8	7,821	-1.3
Seasonal Basin Peak Spring	R	1.5	1,162.3	8,400	4.2
Jeep road and Paradise Lake Trail junction	w, R	2.4	1,164.7	7,591	-3.7

Landmark	Facilities	Diff	S→N	Elev	Gra
Reach a knoll		1.1	1,165.8	8,120	5.2
Mount Lola Trail junction		1.1	1,166.9	7,632	-4.8
White Rock Creek	w	0.1	1,167.0	7,630	-0.2
White Rock Lake Road 19N11A	R	0.7	1,167.7	7,793	2.5
Saddle over Jackson Meadow Reservoir		0.8	1,168.5	8,140	4.7
Cross a road on a viewless saddle	R	0.7	1,169.2	8,032	-1.7
Ridge saddle at the head of Bear Valley		1.0	1,170.2	7,827	-2.2
Meadow Lake Road 19N11 (FS 86)	w, R	2.1	1,172.3	7,523	-1.6
Climb to a ridge		1.1	1,173.4	8,000	4.7
Logging road	R	2.1	1,175.5	7,624	-1.9
Descend to a creek	w	3.8	1,179.3	7,277	-1.0
Minor saddle		0.4	1,179.7	7,135	-3.9
Cross a good road	R	2.1	1,181.8	6,768	-1.9
Junction west of Pass Creek Loop Road	w: 0.30 m W; R	1.8	1,183.6	6,195	-3.5
FS 07 near Jackson Meadow Reservoir	w, R: 0.25 m W	0.3	1,183.9	6,197	0.1
Minor saddle		0.8	1,184.7	6,450	3.4
First (southern) Milton Creek crossing	w	6.0	1,190.7	5,238	-2.2
Bridge over Milton Creek	w	0.8	1,191.5	5,011	-3.1
Wild Plum Road to Wild Plum Campground	R	1.2	1,192.7	4,848	-1.5
Bridge over Haypress Creek	w	0.2	1,192.9	4,733	-6.3
Haypress Creek Trail		0.2	1,193.1	4,815	4.5
Junction after 1001 Mine Creek		0.3	1,193.4	4,808	-0.3
Bridge over North Yuba River	w	1.6	1,195.0	4,601	-1.4
CA 49 near Sierra City	R	0.4	1,195.4	4,591	-0.3
General Delivery Sierra City, CA 96125 530-862-1152	PO, w, G, M, L, r, R: 1.50 m SW	0.0	1,195.4	4,591	-0.3
Switchback up to a flume	w: 0.10 m N	1.8	1,197.2	5,381	4.8

CENTRAL CALIFORNIA

Landmark	Facilities	Diff	S→N	Elev	Gra
Switchback tops off on a ridge		1.5	1,198.7	6,060	4.9
Sierra Buttes jeep trail		3.7	1,202.4	7,143	3.2
Ridgecrest trail junction		1.0	1,203.4	7,400	2.8
Lower Tamarack Lake	w	2.1	1,205.5	6,734	-3.4
Packer Lake saddle		1.5	1,207.0	6,232	-3.6
Packsaddle Campground	w: 0.05 m E	0.2	1,207.2	6,126	-5.8
Unnamed lake's outlet creek	R	1.2	1,208.4	6,485	3.2
Junction to Grass Lake	R	0.6	1,209.0	6,853	6.7
Junction to Deer Lake	R	0.7	1,209.7	7,082	3.6
Join old PCT route		0.7	1,210.4	7,358	4.3
Gold Lake jeep road	w, R: 0.10 m SW	1.3	1,211.7	7,063	-2.5
Jeep road cuts northeast across the crest (alternate routes)	R	1.3	1,213.0	7,333	2.3
Peak 7,541		0.5	1,213.5	7,496	3.5
Cross a trail that heads north		1.6	1,215.1	7,319	-1.2
County-line crest saddle with a diminutive pond, spring nearby (end of alternate route)	w: 0.12 m E	0.9	1,216.0	7,053	-3.2
Cross a jeep road, twice almost touching it	R	1.3	1,217.3	7,353	2.5
Down to a saddle		1.9	1,219.2	6,700	-3.7
A-Tree, focal point for five roads	w, R	0.5	1,219.7	6,550	-3.3
Rise to a saddle after diverging from Cowell Mine Road	R	0.9	1,220.6	6,920	4.5
Saddle south end of McRae Ridge		0.8	1,221.4	7,380	6.3
Near headwaters of West Branch Nelson Creek	w	2.6	1,224.0	6,335	-4.4
Leave West Branch Nelson Creek	w	2.0	1,226.0	5,774	-3.0
Johnsville McRea Road	R	1.1	1,227.1	6,065	2.9
Below Mount Etna proper		2.4	1,229.5	6,768	3.2
South end of Bunker Hill Ridge		0.4	1,229.9	6,745	-0.6

CENTRAL CALIFORNIA

Landmark	Facilities	Diff	S→N	Elev	Gra
Duck Soup Pond, just west of the trail below Bunker Hill Ridge	w	1.3	1,231.2	6,864	1.0
Second saddle next to seasonal springs	w	0.9	1,232.1	6,655	-2.5
Forested slopes to a road	w, R: 0.75 m SW	1.8	1,233.9	6,692	0.2
Quincy–La Porte Road, continue on a level spur road out to a saddle	w, R: 0.25 m SE	0.9	1,234.8	6,454	-2.9
Cross Kenzie Ravine Road 22N60 at a saddle	R	0.8	1,235.6	6,509	0.7
Recross Kenzie Ravine Road 22N60 at another saddle	R	1.8	1,237.4	5,903	-3.7
Cross a jeep road	R	1.2	1,238.6	5,755	-1.3
Chimney Rock		0.8	1,239.4	5,994	3.2
Black Rock Creek Road 22N56 at a saddle	w, R: 0.25 m S	2.0	1,241.4	5,479	-2.8
Junction to Fowler Lake	w: 0.25 m SW	1.1	1,242.5	5,550	0.7
Reach a second road	R	0.3	1,242.8	5,280	-9.8
Cross Sawmill Tom Creek Road 23N65YB	R	1.0	1,243.8	4,973	-3.3
Fowler Creek	w, R: 0.05 m S	0.7	1,244.5	4,940	-0.5
Almost touch the road at a saddle	R	1.1	1,245.6	4,951	0.1
Recross Sawmill Tom Creek Road 23N65YB	R	1.5	1,247.1	4,289	-4.8
Switchback to a spring near Butte Bar Trail junction	w	2.2	1,249.3	3,133	-5.7
Middle Fork Feather River	w	0.4	1,249.7	2,935	-5.4
Deadman Spring saddle		1.3	1,251.0	3,666	6.1
Bear Creek	w	2.0	1,253.0	3,256	-2.2
Switchback to another ridge		2.5	1,255.5	4,250	4.3
Seasonal creek	w	2.3	1,257.8	5,297	4.9
Sunny crest saddle		1.4	1,259.2	5,750	3.5
Seasonal spring	w	0.5	1,259.7	5,832	1.8
Lookout Rock		0.2	1,259.9	5,932	5.4
FS 23N60	R	0.7	1,260.6	5,858	-1.1

CENTRAL CALIFORNIA

Landmark	Facilities	Diff	S→N	Elev	Gra
Road branching north	R	1.3	1,261.9	5,881	0.2
Big Creek Road 33N56 (alternate route)	w: 3.80 m NW; G: 2.70 m NW; M, L: 3.80 m NW; R	1.6	1,263.5	5,502	-2.6
Big Creek	w	2.1	1,265.6	5,528	0.1
Bucks Summit (end of alternate route)		2.3	1,267.9	5,518	0.0
General Delivery Meadow Valley, CA 95956 530-283-1379	PO: 5.20 m E; w, G: 4.10 m E; R	0.0	1,267.9	5,518	0.0
Climb to a switchback	R	1.8	1,269.7	6,315	4.8
Shallow saddle, meet Spanish Peak road	R	2.3	1,272.0	6,898	2.8
Trail junction to Gold Lake Trail		1.2	1,273.2	6,866	-0.3
Cross a jeep road	R	1.1	1,274.3	6,800	-0.7
Descend to a forested saddle		1.0	1,275.3	6,710	-1.0
Headwaters of Clear Creek	w	1.4	1,276.7	6,540	-1.3
Recross Clear Creek	w	1.0	1,277.7	6,211	-3.6
Junction that descends to Three Lakes		1.2	1,278.9	6,236	0.3
Bracken Fern Spring	w, R: 0.10 m S	0.7	1,279.6	6,314	0.4
Canyon View Spring	w, R: 0.05 m W	2.1	1,281.7	5,557	-1.6
Western Pacific's two railroad tracks		4.6	1,286.3	2,313	-8.5
Belden		0.5	1,286.8	2,210	-2.2
CA 70 at Belden Town bridge	R	0.1	1,286.9	2,254	4.8
Belden Town Resort and Lodge Attn: (Your Name) PCT Hiker 14785 Belden Town Road Belden, CA 95915 530-283-9662 Via UPS or FedEx only! $10 fee	w, G, M, L, sh	0.0	1,286.9	2,254	4.8
Caribou Crossroads Campground 16242 CA 70 Belden, CA 95915 530-283-1384; beldentown.com	w, G, M, sh, R: 1.80 m NW	0.0	1,286.9	2,254	4.8

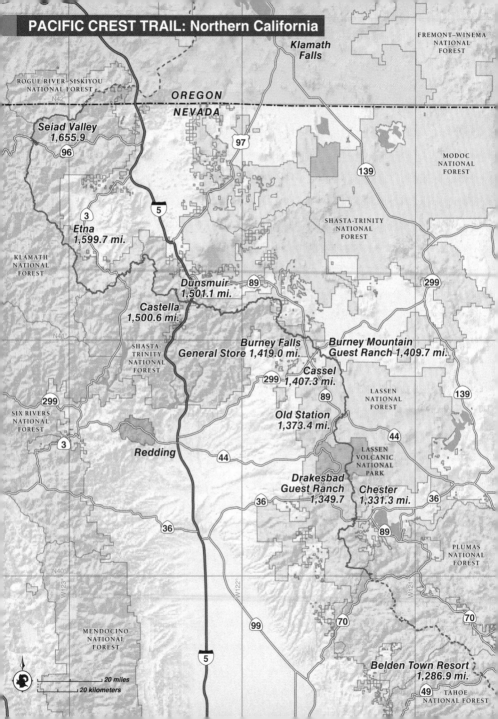

PACIFIC CREST TRAIL: Northern California

FREMONT–WINEMA
NATIONAL
FOREST

Klamath
Falls

ROGUE RIVER–SISKIYOU
NATIONAL FOREST

OREGON
NEVADA

Seiad Valley
1,655.9

MODOC
NATIONAL
FOREST

Etna
1,599.7 mi.

KLAMATH
NATIONAL
FOREST

SHASTA-TRINITY
NATIONAL
FOREST

Dunsmuir
1,501.1 mi.

Castella
1,500.6 mi.

SHASTA-
TRINITY
NATIONAL
FOREST

Burney Falls
General Store 1,419.0 mi.

Burney Mountain
Guest Ranch 1,409.7 mi.

Cassel
1,407.3 mi.

SIX RIVERS
NATIONAL
FOREST

LASSEN
NATIONAL
FOREST

Old Station
1,373.4 mi.

Redding

LASSEN
VOLCANIC
NATIONAL
PARK

Drakesbad
Guest Ranch
1,349.7

Chester
1,331.3 mi.

PLUMAS
NATIONAL
FOREST

MENDOCINO
NATIONAL
FOREST

Belden Town Resort
1,286.9 mi.

TAHOE
NATIONAL FOREST

20 miles
20 kilometers

NORTHERN CALIFORNIA

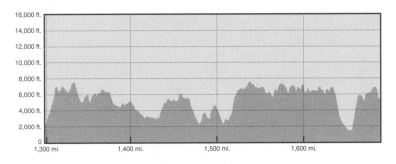

Elevation Profile for Northern California
From Belden to the California–Oregon Border

SEGMENT TOTAL MILEAGE: 404.8 MILES

Landmark	Facilities	Diff	S→N	Elev	Gra
Bridge over Indian Creek	w	1.0	1,287.9	2,375	1.3
Meet a trail after turning west		0.4	1,288.3	2,400	0.7
Junction to an old road, Chips Creek not too far below	R	0.7	1,289.0	2,422	0.3
Williams Cabin Flat, small cabin destroyed by fire on a white-fir-shaded flat	w	3.7	1,292.7	3,624	3.5
Myrtle Flat Camp	w	0.9	1,293.6	4,119	6.0
Flat just before fording Chips Creek	w	1.8	1,295.4	4,739	3.7
Ford Chips Creek	R	0.2	1,295.6	4,725	-0.8
Poison Spring (Andesite Spring)	w	4.0	1,299.6	6,651	5.2
Wide lumber road 26N74	R	0.4	1,300.0	6,890	6.5
Frog Mountain Trail		0.6	1,300.6	7,094	3.7
Frog Spring	w	0.4	1,301.0	6,874	-2.9
Cirby Meadows Road 26N02	R	2.8	1,303.8	6,384	-2.3
Humbug Summit Road 27N11, Cold Springs nearby	w, R: 0.05 m SW	1.6	1,305.4	6,489	0.7
Water Alert (↓): 13.1 m					

Landmark	Facilities	Diff	S→N	Elev	Gra
Past second road 27N11G	R	0.7	1,306.1	6,701	3.3
Pond west of the trail		1.6	1,307.7	7,100	2.7
North end to a jeep road that levels east to Lost Lake	R	0.9	1,308.6	7,000	-1.2
Humboldt Road at Humboldt Summit	R	3.3	1,311.9	6,620	-1.2
Junction to Cub-Butt Divide		1.8	1,313.7	6,454	-1.0
Descend lowest saddle		2.1	1,315.8	6,182	-1.4
Water Alert (↑): 12.7 m					
Carter Creek Trail junction	w: 0.50 m N	2.2	1,318.0	6,620	2.2
Junction to Butt Mountain summit		3.6	1,321.6	7,631	3.0
PCT midpoint milepost		1.6	1,323.2	7,229	-2.7
Shallow gully		1.0	1,324.2	6,920	-3.4
Recross Soldier Creek Springs	w	3.8	1,328.0	5,474	-4.1
Road after private property	R	1.2	1,329.2	5,224	-2.3
Grassy trough		0.9	1,330.1	4,882	-4.1
CA 36	R	1.2	1,331.3	5,051	1.5
St. Bernard Lodge 530-258-3382	w, M, L, sh, R: 1.50 m W	0.0	1,331.3	5,051	1.5
General Delivery Chester, CA 96020 530-258-4184	PO, w, G, M, L, sh, R: 7.50 m NE	0.0	1,331.3	5,051	1.5
Marian Creek, dry most of summer		1.7	1,333.0	5,077	0.2
Stover Camp, spring	w	1.8	1,334.8	5,673	3.6
Cross a major road	R	1.1	1,335.9	5,821	1.5
County-line crest		1.5	1,337.4	5,920	0.7
North Stover Mountain		0.7	1,338.1	6,050	2.0
Cross major logging road 28N61 on a ridge	R	1.6	1,339.7	5,416	-4.3
Bridge over North Fork Feather River	w	1.0	1,340.7	4,998	-4.5
Section Old Red Bluff Road	R	0.9	1,341.6	5,117	1.4

Northern California

NORTHERN CALIFORNIA

Landmark	Facilities	Diff	S→N	Elev	Gra
Descend northwest to an abandoned road	R	4.1	1,345.7	6,055	2.5
Junction to Boundary Spring	w: 0.08 m NE	0.6	1,346.3	5,909	-2.6
Swampy Little Willow Lake		0.2	1,346.5	6,030	6.6
Junction to Terminal Geyser (alternate route 25 yards past junction)		1.0	1,347.5	6,030	0.0
Trail to Drakesbad Guest Ranch		2.2	1,349.7	5,722	-1.5
Drakesbad Guest Ranch Attn: (Your Name) PCT Hiker; include ETA 14423 Chester Warner Valley Road Chester, CA 96020 877-622-0221	w, M, L, sh, R: 0.25 m W	0.0	1,349.7	5,722	-1.5
Warner Valley Campground	w	0.6	1,350.3	5,684	-0.7
Junction to Bench Lake		1.0	1,351.3	6,252	6.2
Kelly Camp Trail		1.3	1,352.6	5,981	-2.3
Kings Creek, junction to Summit Lake	w	0.3	1,352.9	5,998	0.6
Junction to Horseshoe Lake		2.4	1,355.3	6,428	1.9
Second junction that meets the first junction to Horseshoe Lake		1.3	1,356.6	6,684	2.1
Swan Lake's outlet creek	w	0.4	1,357.0	6,617	-1.8
Lower Twin Lake, south end	w	0.6	1,357.6	6,551	-1.2
Junction to Rainbow Lake		0.2	1,357.8	6,547	-0.2
Lower Twin Lake, north end	w	0.2	1,358.0	6,547	0.0
Trail descending left (alternate route)		0.4	1,358.4	6,536	-0.3
Nobles Emigrant Trail		2.4	1,360.8	6,358	-0.8
Opening with view of Soap Lake		1.0	1,361.8	6,320	-0.4
East end of Badger Flat (end of alternate route)		1.6	1,363.4	6,239	-0.5
Junction to a camp, park's north boundary		2.1	1,365.5	6,173	-0.3
Plantation Loop Road 32N42Y	R	1.5	1,367.0	5,569	-4.4
East-west road	R	1.6	1,368.6	5,093	-3.2
Western arm of Plantation Loop Road	R	0.7	1,369.3	4,983	-1.7

Landmark	Facilities	Diff	S→N	Elev	Gra
FS 32N12	R	0.9	1,370.2	4,840	-1.7
Cross a road	R	1.4	1,371.6	4,695	-1.1
Atop a faulted escarpment		0.9	1,372.5	4,720	0.3
North-trending road	R	0.7	1,373.2	4,590	-2.0
Gate across the road to Hat Creek Resort	R	0.2	1,373.4	4,600	0.5
General Delivery Old Station, CA 96071 530-335-7191	PO, w, G, M, L, sh, r, R: 0.30 m N	0.0	1,373.4	4,600	0.5
FS 32N20	R	0.5	1,373.9	4,549	-1.1
FS 32N99	R	0.7	1,374.6	4,539	-0.2
Another crossing of FS 32N99	R	0.3	1,374.9	4,549	0.4
Trail fork to Hat Creek Campground		0.4	1,375.3	4,509	-1.1
FS 33N22	R	1.2	1,376.5	4,384	-1.1
Cross CA 44 near Subway Cave	w, R: 0.5 m SW	0.9	1,377.4	4,366	-0.2
Water Alert (↓): 16.3 m					
Old CA 44	R	1.3	1,378.7	4,371	0.0
CA 44 trailhead	R	1.6	1,380.3	4,879	3.4
Cross usually dry creek gully		1.7	1,382.0	4,640	-1.5
Another dry creek gully		0.8	1,382.8	4,600	-0.5
Shallow depression		1.6	1,384.4	4,820	1.5
Another dry creek gully		1.8	1,386.2	4,801	-0.1
Hat Creek Rim Fire Lookout site		4.5	1,390.7	5,123	0.8
Water Alert (↑): 16.7 m					
FS 22, water tank	w, R: 0.05 m S	2.9	1,393.6	4,659	-1.7
Water Alert (↓): 13.3 m					
Down to a small reservoir, polluted		1.9	1,395.5	4,153	-2.9
Closed gate below FS 36N18	R	3.6	1,399.1	3,944	-0.6
Cross Cassel Fall River Road	R	4.0	1,403.1	3,464	-1.3

Landmark	Facilities	Diff	S→N	Elev	Gra
Cross a dirt road	R	2.1	1,405.2	3,274	-1.0
Water Alert (↑): 13.4 m					
Road above Rock Spring Creek	w, R	1.7	1,406.9	3,036	-1.5
PG&E road south to Cassel	R	0.4	1,407.3	2,990	-1.2
General Delivery Cassel, CA 96016 530-335-3100	PO, w, G, r, R: 1.50 m SW	0.0	1,407.3	2,990	-1.2
Baum Lake Road	R	0.1	1,407.4	3,001	1.2
Junction to Burney Mountain Guest Ranch	R	2.3	1,409.7	3,312	1.5
Burney Mountain Guest Ranch Attn: (Your Name) PCT Hiker 22800 Guest Ranch Road Cassel, CA 96016 530-335-2544 burneymountainguestranch.com for details	w, G, M, L, sh, R: 0.30 m SW	0.0	1,409.7	3,312	1.5
FS 36N33B	R	0.9	1,410.6	3,240	-0.9
CA 299	R	0.7	1,411.3	3,112	-2.0
General Delivery Burney, CA 96013 530-335-5430	PO, w, G, M, L, sh, R: 8.00 m SW	0.0	1,411.3	3,112	-2.0
Slant across a major straight road	R	2.5	1,413.8	3,114	0.0
South edge of Arkright Flat		1.0	1,414.8	2,998	-1.3
Cross a large dirt road	R	0.4	1,415.2	2,996	-0.1
Rim of Lake Road	R	1.3	1,416.5	3,020	0.2
CA 89	R	1.5	1,418.0	2,996	-0.2
Bridge crossing Burney Creek		0.2	1,418.2	2,954	-2.3
Burney Falls, broad path to a parking area on Clark Creek Road		0.8	1,419.0	2,944	-0.1
Burney Falls General Store Attn: (Your Name) PCT Hiker 24900 CA 89 Burney, CA 96013 530-335-5713 $7 fee	w, G, M, sh, r, R: 0.10 m E	0.0	1,419.0	2,944	-0.1
Lake Britton's dam		1.9	1,420.9	2,782	-0.9

Landmark	Facilities	Diff	S→N	Elev	Gra
Rock Creek	w	3.6	1,424.5	2,971	0.6
FS 37N02	R	0.3	1,424.8	3,102	4.7
Cross a road	R	4.5	1,429.3	4,576	3.6
Old clearcut, major logging road		1.1	1,430.4	4,791	2.1
Peavine Creek	w	2.3	1,432.7	4,741	-0.2
Crackling power lines		1.6	1,434.3	5,199	3.1
Road junction at south base of Red Mountain	R	1.2	1,435.5	5,409	1.9
Summit Lake Road 38N10	R	0.6	1,436.1	5,430	0.4
Another spur road	R	0.8	1,436.9	5,321	-1.5
Junction of two roads to Deadman Creek	w, R: 0.50 m E	1.9	1,438.8	5,067	-1.5
Cross Summit Lake Road 38N10 again	R	0.2	1,439.0	5,143	4.1
Descend to a logging road	R	1.5	1,440.5	5,132	-0.1
Descend to a spot with panoramic view		1.8	1,442.3	5,390	1.6
Road splits northeast		1.0	1,443.3	5,311	-0.9
Cross a descending road to a pond		1.2	1,444.5	5,118	-1.7
Back to Summit Lake Road 38N10, just before Bartle Gap		1.5	1,446.0	5,080	-0.3
Cross FS 39N80	R	0.4	1,446.4	5,221	3.8
Moosehead Creek trail, spring	w	0.9	1,447.3	5,273	0.6
Springs at Moosehead Creek's headwaters	w	0.4	1,447.7	5,415	3.9
Rocky point with a view		2.1	1,449.8	6,058	3.3
Cross Summit Lake Road 38N10	R	1.5	1,451.3	6,112	0.4
Tate Creek, resume at a junction with FS 38N10	w, R: 0.50 m N	1.2	1,452.5	5,577	-4.8
Recross FS 38N10	R	1.6	1,454.1	5,524	-0.4
Alder Creek Trail	w: 0.33 m N	1.0	1,455.1	5,403	-1.3
Grizzly Peak Road before Pigeon Hill	R	2.2	1,457.3	5,531	0.6
Recross Grizzly Peak Road	R	0.6	1,457.9	5,420	-2.0

Landmark	Facilities	Diff	S→N	Elev	Gra
South ridge of Grizzly Peak Lookout road	R	2.7	1,460.6	5,654	0.9
Deer Creek	w	2.0	1,462.6	4,690	-5.2
Side canyon with refreshing creek	w	1.1	1,463.7	4,356	-3.3
Butcherknife Creek	w	3.4	1,467.1	3,310	-3.3
Dry Doodlebug Gulch		2.2	1,469.3	3,040	-1.3
FS 38N11	R	1.4	1,470.7	2,440	-4.7
Ash Campground	w	0.2	1,470.9	2,413	-1.5
Fitzhugh Gulch Creek	w	2.2	1,473.1	2,286	-0.6
Ah-Di-Na Campground road, FS 38N53	R	0.5	1,473.6	2,404	2.6
Bald Mountain Road	R	2.9	1,476.5	3,425	3.8
Climb to another road	R	0.8	1,477.3	3,575	2.0
Top a ridge saddle		2.0	1,479.3	3,822	1.3
Trough Creek	w	2.1	1,481.4	3,036	-4.1
Squaw Valley Creek	w	3.3	1,484.7	2,593	-1.5
Southwest to a deep saddle		0.9	1,485.6	3,071	5.8
Girard Ridge Road	R	4.6	1,490.2	4,616	3.6
Northwest-descending ridge		1.6	1,491.8	4,651	0.2
Switchback on a prominent ridge		1.7	1,493.5	4,213	-2.8
South Fork Fall Creek	w	0.5	1,494.0	4,258	1.0
Cross a road, enter Castle Crags State Park	R	2.4	1,496.4	3,742	-2.3
Reach a closed road	R	3.3	1,499.7	2,533	-4.0
Paved Riverside Road (alternate route)	R	0.9	1,500.6	2,154	-4.6
PCT Hiker (Your Name) c/o Ammirati's Market 20107 Castle Creek Road Castella, CA 96017 530-235-2676 Open when post office is closed	w, G, R: 2.00 m SW	0.0	1,500.6	2,154	-4.6

Northern California

Landmark	Facilities	Diff	S→N	Elev	Gra
General Delivery Castella, CA 96017 530-235-4413	PO, w, G, sh, r, R: 2.00 m SW	0.0	1,500.6	2,154	-4.6
Soda Creek Road		0.2	1,500.8	2,084	-3.8
I-5 near Castle Crags State Park, locked gate		0.3	1,501.1	2,131	1.7
General Delivery Dunsmuir, CA 96025 530-235-0338	PO, w, G, M, L, R: 4.50 m N	0.0	1,501.1	2,131	1.7
Locked gate		0.1	1,501.2	2,157	2.8
Kettlebelly Trail (alternate route)		0.5	1,501.7	2,464	6.7
Root Creek Trail	w: 0.25 m N	1.2	1,502.9	2,639	1.6
Leave Root Creek Trail		0.1	1,503.0	2,635	-0.4
Power line saddle		0.2	1,503.2	2,672	2.0
Bobs Hat Trail (end of alternate route)		0.5	1,503.7	2,828	3.4
Winton Canyon Creek	w	1.0	1,504.7	2,848	0.2
East Fork Sulphur Creek	w	2.5	1,507.2	2,694	-0.7
Dog Trail		1.1	1,508.3	3,007	3.1
North Fork Castle Creek tributary	w	1.8	1,510.1	3,123	0.7
Another tributary of North Fork Castle Creek, water upstream	w	1.0	1,511.1	3,437	3.4
Forested saddle just beyond the north boundary of Castle Crags State Park		3.7	1,514.8	5,623	6.4
Cascading creek	w	0.5	1,515.3	5,729	2.3
Densely vegetated creeklet	w	0.9	1,516.2	5,865	1.6
West over to crest saddle 5,983		0.7	1,516.9	5,983	1.8
Ridge		2.0	1,518.9	6,320	1.8
Soapstone Trail		0.5	1,519.4	6,458	3.0
Peak 6,835's south ridge		0.5	1,519.9	6,690	5.0
Trinity Divide	w: 0.33 m E	3.6	1,523.5	6,767	0.2
FS 26 (FS 40N26)	w, R: 0.33 m E	2.3	1,525.8	6,506	-1.2

Landmark	Facilities	Diff	S→N	Elev	Gra
Bear Creek Road 40N45	R	0.8	1,526.6	6,582	1.0
Major saddle		2.1	1,528.7	6,770	1.0
Spring	w	0.3	1,529.0	6,937	6.1
East-dropping ridge with view of Lake Siskiyou		1.9	1,530.9	7,071	0.8
Junction to beautiful Porcupine Lake	w: 0.25 m W	0.4	1,531.3	7,161	2.4
Climbs to a crest, junction to Toad Lake		0.3	1,531.6	7,310	5.4
Trail 6W06		0.9	1,532.5	7,420	1.3
Minor gap on the east ridge		0.9	1,533.4	7,666	3.0
Trail intersection on a windy saddle (alternate route)		1.1	1,534.5	7,411	-2.5
Spur trail to Deadfall Lakes	w	2.2	1,536.7	7,222	-0.9
Cross Deadfall Lakes Trail		0.3	1,537.0	7,230	0.3
Gully		1.2	1,538.2	7,080	-1.4
Parks Creek Road 42N17, shallow crest saddle (end of alternate route)	R	1.5	1,539.7	6,860	-1.6
Tops out on an adjacent ridge		4.6	1,544.3	6,650	-0.8
Chilcoot Creek, spring-fed creeklet nearby	w	1.6	1,545.9	6,650	0.0
Bull Lake crest saddle, meet old Sisson-Callahan Trail		2.1	1,548.0	7,059	2.1
Secondary crest saddle		1.6	1,549.6	6,770	-2.0
Fen Nature Trail		0.9	1,550.5	6,514	-3.1
Cooper Meadows Trail		1.3	1,551.8	6,180	-2.8
Descend to another saddle		1.0	1,552.8	6,045	-1.5
Meet two springs	w	1.3	1,554.1	6,055	0.1
Cross a secondary ridge		1.1	1,555.2	6,100	0.4
Masterson Meadow	w	0.6	1,555.8	6,135	0.6
Grouse Creek Trail		0.2	1,556.0	6,110	-1.4
Masterson Meadow Lake's seasonal creek	w	1.1	1,557.1	6,174	0.6

Landmark	Facilities	Diff	S→N	Elev	Gra
Rocky knoll on a ridge		1.3	1,558.4	6,170	0.0
FS 40N08		1.6	1,560.0	5,472	-4.7
CA 3 at Scott Mountain Summit	w, R: 0.25 m S	0.2	1,560.2	5,407	-3.5
Enter Trinity Alps Wilderness		2.6	1,562.8	6,382	4.1
Shallow crest gap		1.2	1,564.0	6,683	2.7
Spring	w	0.7	1,564.7	6,440	-3.8
FS 40N63	R	1.2	1,565.9	6,234	-1.9
Mosquito Lake creek	w	0.1	1,566.0	6,295	6.6
Youth summer camp's primitive trail		0.6	1,566.6	6,567	4.9
Junction to East Boulder and Marshy Lakes		1.5	1,568.1	7,020	3.3
Edge of talus slope		1.3	1,569.4	7,240	1.8
East end of a windswept crest		0.7	1,570.1	7,426	2.9
Another meadow		0.4	1,570.5	7,260	-4.5
Trail to Telephone Lake	w: 0.70 m W	0.2	1,570.7	7,253	-0.4
North end of a crest saddle, junction with Bloody Run Trail 8W04		0.8	1,571.5	7,139	-1.5
On the crest with view of West Boulder Creek canyon		0.6	1,572.1	7,300	2.9
Sage-covered crest saddle		0.4	1,572.5	7,183	-3.2
Trail 8W03		1.2	1,573.7	7,132	-0.5
Crest, junction with Trail 8W07 near Section Line Lake		0.3	1,574.0	7,230	3.5
Swath of alders	w	1.5	1,575.5	6,850	-2.9
Crest saddle with Trail 9W03		1.1	1,576.6	6,780	-0.6
Saddle's west end, another branch of Trail 9W03		0.2	1,576.8	6,793	0.7
South Fork Ridge Trail		0.2	1,577.0	6,685	-5.9
Alder-lined creeklet	w	1.1	1,578.1	6,254	-4.3
South Fork Lakes Trail		0.8	1,578.9	5,841	-5.6

Landmark	Facilities	Diff	S→N	Elev	Gra
South Fork Scott River	w	0.1	1,579.0	5,782	-6.4
Another alder-lined creeklet	w	0.5	1,579.5	5,927	3.1
FS 93 at Carter Meadows Summit	R	0.6	1,580.1	6,178	4.5
Cross a jeep road		0.2	1,580.3	6,303	6.8
Crest saddle with views of South Fork Lakes canyon		0.8	1,581.1	6,720	5.7
Under a crest saddle		1.7	1,582.8	6,910	1.2
Climb to a jeep trail		2.2	1,585.0	6,940	0.1
Jeep trail to Siphon Lake	w: 0.75 m W	0.2	1,585.2	7,075	7.3
Peak 7,383		0.3	1,585.5	7,274	7.2
Enter Klamath National Forest Russian Wilderness		0.6	1,586.1	7,148	-2.3
Bingham Lake's outlet creek under boulders		0.9	1,587.0	6,901	-3.0
Bedrock water chute, usually dry		1.9	1,588.9	6,410	-2.8
Alder-choked creek	w	0.4	1,589.3	6,700	7.9
Blakes Fork Creek under boulders		0.5	1,589.8	6,700	0.0
Curve northeast, 250 feet below Statue Lake, water from creek	w	1.0	1,590.8	6,904	2.2
Duck Lakes Trail		1.1	1,591.9	6,703	-2.0
Paynes Lake Creek	w	2.1	1,594.0	6,518	-1.0
Glacial bowl	w	0.7	1,594.7	6,652	2.1
Junction to Taylor Lake		1.5	1,596.2	7,057	2.9
Enter Klamath National Forest	R	0.2	1,596.4	7,178	6.6
Jeep-road junction to Upper Ruffey Lake	R	1.7	1,598.1	6,873	-1.9
Sawyers Bar Road at Etna Summit	R	1.6	1,599.7	5,980	-6.1
General Delivery Etna, CA 96027 530-467-3981	PO, w, G, M, L, sh, R: 10.50 m NE	0.0	1,599.7	5,980	-6.1
Enter Marble Mountain Wilderness		1.9	1,601.6	6,342	2.1
Southeast end of Razor Ridge		1.8	1,603.4	6,714	2.2

Landmark	Facilities	Diff	S→N	Elev	Gra
Cross a more persistent creeklet	w	1.0	1,604.4	6,450	-2.9
Reach another creek	w	2.0	1,606.4	6,170	-1.5
Headwaters of Babs Fork Kidder Creek	w: 0.20 m E	0.8	1,607.2	6,316	2.0
Saddle just north of Peak 6,667		1.5	1,608.7	6,430	0.8
Shelly Lake's outlet creek	w	1.6	1,610.3	6,187	-1.6
Shelly Meadows	w	0.1	1,610.4	6,239	5.7
Shelly Fork Trail		0.4	1,610.8	6,333	2.6
Saddle below Peak 7,095		2.2	1,613.0	6,410	0.4
Creeklet	w	0.5	1,613.5	6,279	-2.8
Fisher Lake	w	0.3	1,613.8	6,220	-2.1
Marten Lake	w	0.2	1,614.0	6,327	5.8
Junction to older PCT route to Kidder Lake Trail		1.2	1,615.2	6,478	1.4
Conspicuous saddle		0.5	1,615.7	6,870	8.5
Junction with older PCT segment		1.2	1,616.9	7,075	1.9
Saddle, meet Shackleford Creek Trail		1.6	1,618.5	6,590	-3.3
Junction with Red Rock Valley and Cold Spring Trails		1.6	1,620.1	6,157	-2.9
Second set of trails to Red Rock Valley Trail/ west Cold Spring Trail	w: 0.25 m S	0.3	1,620.4	6,370	7.7
Shadow Lake Trail		0.3	1,620.7	6,504	4.9
Soft Water Spring		0.8	1,621.5	6,539	0.5
Junction to Sky High Lakes Trail		0.7	1,622.2	6,446	-1.4
Junction to Big Elk Lake		0.5	1,622.7	6,229	-4.7
Return junction to Sky High Lakes Trail		0.4	1,623.1	5,908	-8.7
Marble Valley Guard Station/ Canyon Creek Trail	w	0.6	1,623.7	5,729	-3.2
Marble Gap Trail		0.4	1,624.1	5,886	4.3
Junction to Big Rock Camp		2.2	1,626.3	6,640	3.7

Landmark	Facilities	Diff	S→N	Elev	Gra
Jumpoff, a low point on a narrow crest		0.3	1,626.6	6,657	0.6
Notch in southwest end of Cayenne Ridge		2.3	1,628.9	6,186	-2.2
Paradise Lake	w	0.1	1,629.0	6,144	-4.6
Junction to Bear and Turk Lakes		1.6	1,630.6	6,564	2.8
Big Ridge Cutoff Trail, views		0.7	1,631.3	6,738	2.7
Buckhorn Spring	w	3.2	1,634.5	6,567	-0.6
Small flat		0.3	1,634.8	6,300	-9.7
Huckleberry Mountain Trail		1.0	1,635.8	6,020	-3.0
North boundary of Marble Mountain Wilderness	R	0.3	1,636.1	5,991	-1.0
Cross a good road near Cold Spring Trailhead	R	1.3	1,637.4	5,359	-5.3
Cross another good road	R	1.2	1,638.6	4,816	-4.9
Last logging road crossing	R	0.8	1,639.4	4,321	-6.7
Grider Creek Trail at FS 46N72/ Cold Spring Creek	w, R	2.1	1,641.5	3,244	-5.6
FS 45N72X		0.2	1,641.7	3,180	-3.5
Footbridge across Grider Creek	w	0.8	1,642.5	2,891	-3.9
Second footbridge across Grider Creek	w	1.2	1,643.7	2,664	-2.1
Third footbridge across Grider Creek	w	1.7	1,645.4	2,332	-2.1
Bark Shanty Creek	w	0.4	1,645.8	2,347	0.4
Old Grider Creek Trail		1.9	1,647.7	2,004	-2.0
Grider Creek Trail at Grider Creek Campground		1.8	1,649.5	1,704	-1.8
FS 46N66	R	0.3	1,649.8	1,751	1.7
Last bridge across Grider Creek	w	0.8	1,650.6	1,560	-2.6
Junction with a spur road	R	1.5	1,652.1	1,405	-1.1
CA 96	R	2.4	1,654.5	1,420	0.1
Klamath River		0.5	1,655.0	1,378	-0.9

Northern California

Landmark	Facilities	Diff	S→N	Elev	Gra
CA 96 at Seiad Valley	R	0.9	1,655.9	1,373	-0.1
General Delivery Seiad Valley, CA 96086 530-496-3211	PO, w, G, M, r, R	0.0	1,655.9	1,373	-0.1
Schoolhouse Creek		0.5	1,656.4	1,380	0.2
Lower Devils Peak Lookout Trail 12W04		0.3	1,656.7	1,372	-0.3
Junction to a trail paralleling CA 96	R	0.2	1,656.9	1,556	10.0
Fern Spring	w	0.7	1,657.6	1,935	5.9
Lookout Spring	w	4.2	1,661.8	4,882	7.6
Lower Devils Peak saddle		0.2	1,662.0	5,004	6.6
Unmaintained southeast-heading trail		0.6	1,662.6	5,133	2.3
Upper Devils Peak's western arm		1.0	1,663.6	5,782	7.1
Portuguese Creek Trail 12W03	w: 0.15 m W	1.2	1,664.8	5,797	0.1
Boundary Trail 12W47		0.4	1,665.2	5,894	2.6
Spring in spongy ground	w	0.8	1,666.0	5,715	-2.4
Kangaroo Mountain's east ridge		0.5	1,666.5	5,900	4.0
Spur trail to a jeep road	R	0.2	1,666.7	5,904	0.2
Cross the jeep road	R	1.0	1,667.7	5,674	-2.5
Junction with Horse Camp Trail 958 to Echo Lake		0.6	1,668.3	5,877	3.7
Cook and Green Pass	w: 0.10 m NW	2.5	1,670.8	4,736	-5.0
Trail 11W02		2.7	1,673.5	6,040	5.2
Horse Creek Trail 11W01		2.2	1,675.7	6,056	0.1
Junction to Tin Cup Trail		0.2	1,675.9	6,062	0.3
Junction with the old PCT	w: 0.10 m SW	2.0	1,677.9	5,933	-0.7
FS 47N81	R	2.3	1,680.2	6,234	1.4
Junction to Alex Hole Spring	w: 0.25 m N	3.0	1,683.2	6,588	1.3
Mud Springs spur road	w, R: 0.20 m NW	2.1	1,685.3	6,732	0.7

Landmark	Facilities	Diff	S→N	Elev	Gra
Misnamed Big Rock	R	0.8	1,686.1	6,674	-0.8
FS 40S01	R	0.9	1,687.0	6,271	-4.9
Road north of Bearground Spring	w, R	0.6	1,687.6	5,980	-5.3
Wards Fork Gap		1.5	1,689.1	5,287	-5.0
Bridge over Donomore Creek	w	1.4	1,690.5	5,585	2.3

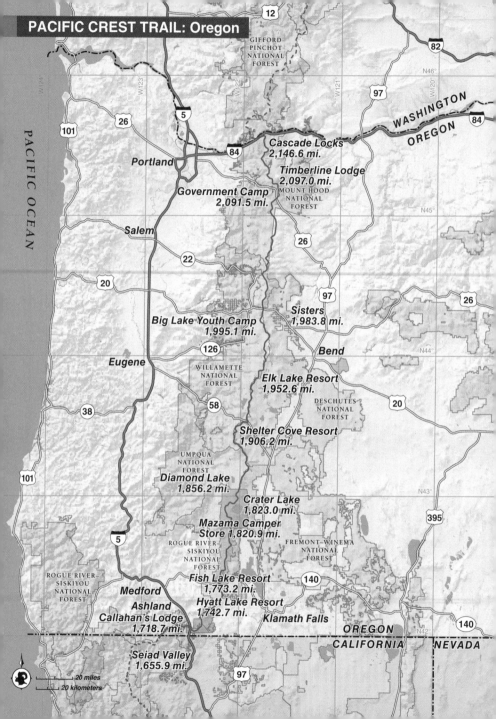

PACIFIC CREST TRAIL: Oregon

PACIFIC OCEAN

WASHINGTON
OREGON

GIFFORD PINCHOT NATIONAL FOREST

Portland

Cascade Locks
2,146.6 mi.

Timberline Lodge
2,097.0 mi.

MOUNT HOOD NATIONAL FOREST

Government Camp
2,091.5 mi.

Salem

Sisters
1,983.8 mi.

Big Lake Youth Camp
1,995.1 mi.

Bend

WILLAMETTE NATIONAL FOREST

Eugene

Elk Lake Resort
1,952.6 mi.

DESCHUTES NATIONAL FOREST

Shelter Cove Resort
1,906.2 mi.

UMPQUA NATIONAL FOREST

Diamond Lake
1,856.2 mi.

Crater Lake
1,823.0 mi.

Mazama Camper
Store 1,820.9 mi.

ROGUE RIVER–SISKIYOU NATIONAL FOREST

FREMONT–WINEMA NATIONAL FOREST

Fish Lake Resort
1,773.2 mi.

Hyatt Lake Resort
1,742.7 mi.

Medford

Ashland

Klamath Falls

Callahan's Lodge
1,718.7 mi.

ROGUE RIVER–SISKIYOU NATIONAL FOREST

OREGON
CALIFORNIA   NEVADA

Seiad Valley
1,655.9 mi.

20 miles
20 kilometers

OREGON

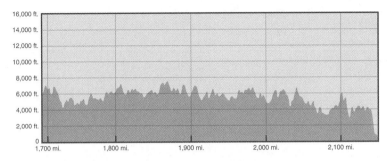

Elevation Profile for Oregon
From the California–Oregon Border to the Oregon–Washington Border

SEGMENT TOTAL MILEAGE: 455.5 MILES

Landmark	Facilities	Diff	S→N	Elev	Gra
California–Oregon border		1.2	1,691.7	6,068	4.4
Logging road saddle, cross FS 2025	R	0.3	1,692.0	6,190	4.4
West ridge of twin-topped Observation Peak		1.6	1,693.6	6,731	3.7
Observation Gap		1.1	1,694.7	7,048	3.1
Jackson Gap		1.1	1,695.8	6,975	-0.7
Spur road to Sheep Camp Spring	w, R	0.3	1,696.1	6,866	-3.9
Water Alert (↓):	12.3 m				
Wrangle Gap		2.2	1,698.3	6,499	-1.8
Siskiyou Gap		3.7	1,702.0	5,904	-1.7
Cross FS 40S12	R	0.3	1,702.3	5,800	-3.8
Five-way road junction on Long John Saddle	R	1.3	1,703.6	5,892	0.8
Open crest saddle		2.0	1,705.6	6,710	4.2
Cross a spur road	R	0.6	1,706.2	6,888	3.9
Another saddle		1.2	1,707.4	6,981	0.8
Water Alert (↑):	12.1 m				

Oregon

Landmark	Facilities	Diff	S→N	Elev	Gra
Grouse Gap, FS 40S30	w, R: 0.20 m S	0.8	1,708.2	6,604	-5.1
Cross FS 40S15 to Mount Ashland Campground	w, R: 0.50 m NE	1.8	1,710.0	6,513	-0.5
Cross FS 20	R	1.6	1,711.6	6,175	-2.3
FS 2080	R	0.3	1,711.9	6,054	-4.4
General Delivery Ashland, OR 97520 541-552-1622	PO, w, G, M, L, R: 12.40 m N	0.0	1,711.9	6,054	-4.4
Saddle below the former Mount Ashland Inn		1.5	1,713.4	5,472	-4.1
Another saddle		0.7	1,714.1	5,140	-5.4
Another saddle with four roads	R	0.9	1,715.0	5,037	-1.2
Spring-fed gully	w	2.1	1,717.1	4,888	-0.8
Road past the spring-fed gully	R	0.4	1,717.5	4,566	-8.6
Cross another road	R	0.1	1,717.6	4,493	-11.0
Cross a third road	R	0.1	1,717.7	4,360	-12.0
Path ends at abandoned segment of Old US 99	R	0.8	1,718.5	4,250	-1.5
Old US 99, just below I-5 near Mount Ashland Road	R	0.2	1,718.7	4,207	-2.3
(Your Name) PCT Hiker c/o Callahan's Mountain Lodge 7100 Old US 99 S Ashland, OR 97520 541-482-1299; callahanslodge.com $5 fee	w, M, L, sh, R: 0.90 m N	0.0	1,718.7	4,207	-2.3
General Delivery Ashland, OR 97520 541-552-1622	PO, w, G, M, L, R: 12.90 m N	0.0	1,718.7	4,207	-2.3
Cross under I-5		0.2	1,718.9	4,271	3.5
Resumption of PCT after I-5		0.4	1,719.3	4,357	2.3
Y-junction		2.1	1,721.4	4,897	2.8
Major intersection		0.3	1,721.7	4,834	-2.3
Minor road		1.7	1,723.4	5,112	1.8

OREGON

Landmark	Facilities	Diff	S→N	Elev	Gra
Pilot Rock Trail	R	0.1	1,723.5	5,155	4.7
Reach the first gate		0.9	1,724.4	5,160	0.1
Crest saddle		0.7	1,725.1	5,020	-2.2
Leave Soda Mountain Wilderness		0.3	1,725.4	4,937	-3.0
North to a crest		0.9	1,726.3	5,019	1.0
Trail's resumption on the left		0.2	1,726.5	5,060	2.2
Enter Soda Mountain Wilderness	R	0.2	1,726.7	5,221	8.8
Lone Pilot Trail	R	0.2	1,726.9	5,307	4.7
Very refreshing fenced-in spring	w	1.2	1,728.1	5,330	0.2
Descend northeast to a saddle		0.4	1,728.5	5,140	-5.2
South slope of Little Pilot Peak		0.8	1,729.3	5,551	5.6
Spring-fed tub, 80 yards northwest down from the trail	w	0.8	1,730.1	5,475	-1.0
Meet an old trail		0.2	1,730.3	5,560	4.6
Shaded saddle		0.6	1,730.9	5,420	-2.5
Soda Mountain Road	R	0.5	1,731.4	5,291	-2.8
Hobart Bluff spur trail		0.9	1,732.3	5,284	-0.1
OR 66 at Green Springs Summit	w, R: 0.25 m NE	3.3	1,735.6	4,558	-2.4
One-lane road past a small power line	R	1.2	1,736.8	4,700	1.3
Old Hyatt Prairie Road	R	0.2	1,737.0	4,705	0.3
BLM 39-3E-32	R	0.4	1,737.4	4,812	2.9
Cross BLM 39-3E-32	w	2.4	1,739.8	4,735	-0.3
Ashland lateral canal, dry gully		0.3	1,740.1	4,600	-4.9
Second gully meets a trail to Little Hyatt Reservoir	w: 0.25 m N	1.0	1,741.1	4,618	0.2
Old Hyatt Prairie Road	R	0.1	1,741.2	4,623	0.5
Hyatt Lake Campground spur trail, past old roads to a road fork	R	1.5	1,742.7	5,105	3.5

OREGON

Landmark	Facilities	Diff	S→N	Elev	Gra
Hyatt Lake Resort Attn: (Your Name) PCT Hiker 7900 Hyatt Prairie Road Ashland, OR 97520 541-482-3331; hyattlake.com Via UPS only!	w, G, M, sh, r, R: 0.75 m N	0.0	1,742.7	5,105	3.5
BLM 39-3E-15	R	2.0	1,744.7	5,121	0.1
Wildcat Glades Road 39-4E-19.3	R	0.9	1,745.6	5,086	-0.4
Cross an older road to Wildcat Glades and reach a seeping creek	R	0.5	1,746.1	5,198	2.4
Reaches the main summit		0.7	1,746.8	5,510	4.8
Almost touch a saddle		0.5	1,747.3	5,310	-4.3
Cross Eve Springs Road, which climbs southwest to a rock quarry	R	2.0	1,749.3	4,617	-3.8
Junction to Soda Creek	w: 0.50 m S	0.1	1,749.4	4,626	1.0
Secondary road climbs east	R	0.1	1,749.5	4,621	-0.5
Cross a little-used road to Klum Landing County Campground	w, sh, R: 0.30 m E	0.9	1,750.4	4,705	1.0
Drops northeast to a well-maintained road	R	0.3	1,750.7	4,635	-2.5
Grizzly Creek	w	0.5	1,751.2	4,459	-3.8
Moon Prairie Road	R	0.4	1,751.6	4,587	3.5
Keno Access Road	R	0.8	1,752.4	4,748	2.2
Old road before the newer logging road	R	0.2	1,752.6	4,790	2.3
Brush Mountain Road	R	0.5	1,753.1	4,987	4.3
Old logging road	R	1.6	1,754.7	5,501	3.5
Approach Big Draw Road 2520	w, R: 0.05 m E	0.5	1,755.2	5,708	4.5
Parallel Big Draw Road 2520 to a crossing, east to Big Springs creeklet	w, R: 0.10 m E	0.2	1,755.4	5,715	0.4
Rogue River–Siskiyou National Forest boundary		1.7	1,757.1	6,162	2.9
Faint spur trail to FS 650	R	1.0	1,758.1	5,880	-3.1
Cross a closed road	R	1.2	1,759.3	5,390	-4.4

OREGON

Landmark	Facilities	Diff	S→N	Elev	Gra
Cross FS 800	R	0.3	1,759.6	5,398	0.3
Dead Indian Memorial Road	R	2.0	1,761.6	5,383	-0.1
Junction to South Brown Mountain Shelter	w: 0.10 m W	1.7	1,763.3	5,305	-0.5
Cross FS 700	R	0.2	1,763.5	5,268	-2.0
Brown Mountain Trail, South Fork Little Butte Creek		2.0	1,765.5	5,234	-0.2
Minor ridge		1.5	1,767.0	5,240	0.0
High Lakes Bike Trail 6200	w: 0.33 m W	6.2	1,773.2	4,952	-0.5
Fish Lake Resort Attn: (Your Name) PCT Hiker OR 140, Mile Marker 30 Eagle Point, OR 97524 541-949-8500; fishlakeresort.net	w, G, M, sh, R: 1.60 m W	0.0	1,773.2	4,952	-0.5
OR 140 near Fish Lake	R	0.2	1,773.4	4,970	1.0
Junction to large trailhead parking lot	w	0.4	1,773.8	5,094	3.4
Enter Sky Lakes Wilderness		0.4	1,774.2	5,221	3.4
Join Mount McLoughlin Trail 3716		3.0	1,777.2	6,095	3.2
Freye Lake spur trail	w: 0.25 m N	0.3	1,777.5	6,190	3.4
Leave Mount McLoughlin Trail, westbound		0.2	1,777.7	6,251	3.3
Twin Ponds Trail to Summit Lake	w: 0.40 m NW	3.8	1,781.5	5,840	-1.2
Cat Hill Way Trail 992		1.5	1,783.0	6,079	1.7
Broad saddle		1.6	1,784.6	6,300	1.5
Another saddle, junction to Christis Spring	w: 0.03 m N	0.3	1,784.9	6,290	-0.4
Red Lake Trail 987		1.9	1,786.8	6,035	-1.5
North junction of Red Lake Trail 987		2.7	1,789.5	6,067	0.1
Sky Lakes Trail 3762		0.9	1,790.4	6,158	1.1
Spur trail to overlook		2.5	1,792.9	6,619	2.0
Sky Lakes Cutoff Trail		0.8	1,793.7	6,580	-0.5
Divide Trail 3717		1.2	1,794.9	6,815	2.1

Oregon

OREGON

Landmark	Facilities	Diff	S→N	Elev	Gra
Hemlock Lake Trail 985		1.0	1,795.9	6,600	-2.3
Snow Lakes Trail 3739	w: 0.20 m NE	0.1	1,796.0	6,693	10.1
Devils Peak Trail 984		1.7	1,797.7	7,232	3.4
Abandoned segment of Devils Peak Trail		0.2	1,797.9	7,190	-2.3
Devils Peak–Lee Peak saddle		0.5	1,798.4	7,320	2.8
Junction to Seven Lakes Trail 981		2.4	1,800.8	6,246	-4.9
Seven Lakes Trail 981		0.7	1,801.5	6,159	-1.3
Honeymoon Creek	w	0.6	1,802.1	5,992	-3.0
Sevenmile Trail 3703		2.1	1,804.2	5,811	-0.9
Meet Middle Fork Basin Trail to Ranger Springs	w: 0.80 m W	0.1	1,804.3	5,763	-5.2
Big Bunchgrass Trail 1089A		1.0	1,805.3	6,020	2.8
McKie Camp Trail 1089		1.1	1,806.4	6,327	3.0
Jack Spring spur trail	w: 0.50 m NW	2.5	1,808.9	6,205	-0.5
Water Alert (↓):	13.8 m				
South end of Stuart Falls Trail 1078		1.6	1,810.5	6,061	-1.2
Second old, closed road	R	5.5	1,816.0	6,311	0.5
Top of narrow, open flat		2.4	1,818.4	6,503	0.9
OR 62, close to Mazama Campground	w, G, sh, R: 1.00 m SE	2.5	1,820.9	6,177	-1.4
PCT Hiker (Your Name); include ETA c/o Mazama Camper Store 700 Mazama Village Dr. Crater Lake, OR 97604 541-594-2255 Via UPS or FedEx only!	w, G, M, sh, R: 1.00 m SE	0.0	1,820.9	6,177	-1.4
General Delivery Crater Lake, OR 97604 541-594-3115 (call to confirm)	PO, w, G, M, L, R: 6.90 m NE	0.0	1,820.9	6,177	-1.4
Annie Spring Cutoff Trail in a second fault-line gully		0.8	1,821.7	6,336	2.2
Water Alert (↑):	14.3 m				

Landmark	Facilities	Diff	S→N	Elev	Gra
Castle Creek	w	1.0	1,822.7	6,134	-2.2
Dutton Creek Trail (alternate hikers' PCT via Rim Village)		0.3	1,823.0	6,093	-1.5
General Delivery Crater Lake, OR 97604 541-594-3115 (call to confirm)	PO, w, G, M, L: 2.80 m SE	0.0	1,823.0	6,093	-1.5
Dutton Creek	w	0.1	1,823.1	6,075	-2.0
Trapper Creek	w	1.1	1,824.2	5,968	-0.9
Bybee Creek	w: 0.75 m W	2.2	1,826.4	5,965	0.0
Junction to Lightning Springs	w: 0.75 m W	1.0	1,827.4	5,869	-0.9
Junction to stock camps		1.2	1,828.6	5,608	-2.4
South Fork of Copeland Creek	w	0.9	1,829.5	5,458	-1.8
Middle Fork of Copeland Creek	w	0.2	1,829.7	5,485	1.5
Sphagnum Bog Trail		4.7	1,834.4	6,088	1.4
Junction to Red Cone Springs	w: 0.10 m E	0.9	1,835.3	6,240	1.8
Water Alert (↓): 20.8 m					
Bald Crater Loop Trail		0.6	1,835.9	6,129	-2.0
Small parking area along North Entrance Road	R	3.3	1,839.2	6,496	1.2
Cross Rim Drive (end of alternate hikers' PCT)		0.1	1,839.3	6,473	-2.5
Walk east to a road fork and branch northeast	R	2.7	1,842.0	5,996	-1.9
Back on trail tread		1.3	1,843.3	6,146	1.3
North boundary of Crater Lake National Park		2.7	1,846.0	5,942	-0.8
OR 138 near the Cascade Crest	R	1.8	1,847.8	5,923	-0.1
South end of North Crater Trail 1410 (alternate route if resupplying at Diamond Lake)		0.2	1,848.0	5,898	-1.4
Old, abandoned Summit Rock Road	R	0.4	1,848.4	5,946	1.3
Enter Mount Thielsen Wilderness		0.6	1,849.0	6,004	1.0
Mount Thielsen Trail 1456		4.9	1,853.9	7,334	2.9

Oregon

Landmark	Facilities	Diff	S→N	Elev	Gra
Head to northwest ridge of Mount Thielsen peak		1.0	1,854.9	7,370	0.4
Water Alert (↑): 20.9 m					
Thielsen Creek	w	1.2	1,856.1	6,925	-4.0
Water Alert (↓): 16.3 m					
Thielsen Creek Trail 1449		0.1	1,856.2	6,950	2.7
General Delivery Diamond Lake, OR 97731 541-365-4411	PO, w, G, M, L, R: 5.60 m W	0.0	1,856.2	6,950	2.7
Pumice Flat		2.2	1,858.4	7,133	0.9
Howlock Mountain Trail 1448		0.7	1,859.1	7,291	2.5
Climb to a crest saddle		0.4	1,859.5	7,415	3.4
Highest point in Oregon–Washington PCT segment		1.3	1,860.8	7,572	1.3
Northeast of saddle past Tipsoo Peak		0.8	1,861.6	7,300	-3.7
Maidu Lake Trail 1446	w: 0.90 m NW	4.3	1,865.9	6,203	-2.8
Crossing of county-line ridge		1.4	1,867.3	6,515	2.4
Descend to a crest saddle		2.3	1,869.6	6,525	0.0
Diagonal northeast to a saddle		1.9	1,871.5	6,300	-1.3
Water Alert (↑): 16.0 m					
Tolo Camp, junction to Six Horse Spring	w: 0.33 m E	0.6	1,872.1	6,218	-1.5
Traverse over to another saddle		0.6	1,872.7	6,325	1.9
Tolo Creek Trail 1466		1.5	1,874.2	6,605	2.0
Spur trail to Windigo Pass Trailhead, parking area by old Cascade Lakes Road	R	3.7	1,877.9	5,845	-2.2
Windigo Pass, FS 60 (alternate route)	R	0.4	1,878.3	5,821	-0.7
Minor crest saddle to lakelet	w: 0.10 m NW	2.2	1,880.5	6,588	3.8
Saddle by southwest ridge of Cowhorn Mountain		1.7	1,882.2	7,100	3.3
Forested bowl		3.1	1,885.3	6,380	-2.4

Oregon

OREGON

Landmark	Facilities	Diff	S→N	Elev	Gra
Summit Lake's south shore	w	3.9	1,889.2	5,560	-2.3
FS 6010	R	0.2	1,889.4	5,570	0.5
Emigrant Pass Road 380 near Summit Lake Campground	R	1.3	1,890.7	5,604	0.3
Leaving west shore of last in a series of lakes	w	1.1	1,891.8	5,670	0.7
South shore of an accessible lake	w	0.7	1,892.5	5,888	3.4
Crater Butte and Rockpile Trails		1.2	1,893.7	6,184	2.7
Northwest up a switchback, plenty of ponds north on PCT		1.3	1,895.0	6,600	3.5
North shore of green Lils Lake, plenty of ponds south on PCT	w	6.8	1,901.8	6,020	-0.9
Descend to even larger Hidden Lake	w	0.6	1,902.4	5,854	-3.0
Junction to well-hidden Midnight Lake	w: 0.05 m E	2.4	1,904.8	5,386	-2.1
Pengra Pass		1.4	1,906.2	5,021	-2.8
Shelter Cove Resort Attn: (Your Name) PCT Hiker 27600 West Odell Lake Road Crescent Lake, OR 97733 541-433-2548 Via UPS only!	PO, w, G, M, sh, r, R: 1.50 m SE	0.0	1,906.2	5,021	-2.8
Old Oregon Skyline Trail (end of alternate route)		0.4	1,906.6	5,066	1.2
OR 58 near Willamette Pass	R	1.3	1,907.9	5,088	0.2
Trailhead-parking spur trail		0.2	1,908.1	5,132	2.4
Taits Loop		2.4	1,910.5	5,669	2.4
Ridge above South (Lower) Rosary Lake	w	0.2	1,910.7	5,720	2.8
Middle Rosary Lake	w	0.7	1,911.4	5,830	1.7
Divide between Middle and North Rosary Lakes	w	0.1	1,911.5	5,848	2.0
North Rosary Lake	w	0.2	1,911.7	5,830	-1.0
Water Alert (↓): 13.5 m					
Maiden Lake Trail 3841		0.4	1,912.1	5,994	4.5

OREGON

Landmark	Facilities	Diff	S→N	Elev	Gra
Switchback west to a saddle at Willamette National Forest boundary		0.5	1,912.6	6,173	3.9
Minor saddle		1.3	1,913.9	6,070	-0.9
Maiden Peak Loop Snow Trail		0.5	1,914.4	6,039	-0.7
Maiden Peak Trail 3681		0.9	1,915.3	5,634	-4.9
Bobby Lake Trail 3663 and Moore Creek Trail 3840		2.3	1,917.6	5,469	-0.8
Climb northwest to a saddle		1.6	1,919.2	5,980	3.5
Twins Trail 3595		1.2	1,920.4	6,264	2.6
Cluster of three ponds		2.4	1,922.8	6,320	0.3
Water Alert (↑): 13.4 m					
Charlton Lake Trail 3593	w: 0.10 m SE	2.3	1,925.1	5,737	-2.8
FS 5897	R	0.5	1,925.6	5,799	1.3
Lily Lake Trail 19	w: 0.75 m NE	1.4	1,927.0	6,006	1.6
Taylor Lake	w	3.3	1,930.3	5,550	-1.5
FS 600 at Irish Lake	w, R	0.3	1,930.6	5,563	0.5
Enter Three Sisters Wilderness		0.1	1,930.7	5,578	1.6
Riffle Lake	w	0.8	1,931.5	5,581	0.0
Climb to a higher ridge		1.2	1,932.7	5,730	1.3
East shore of Brahma Lake	w	0.6	1,933.3	5,672	-1.0
Jezebel Lake	w	1.0	1,934.3	5,857	2.0
Stormy Lake	w	1.0	1,935.3	6,057	2.2
Blaze Lake	w	0.4	1,935.7	5,950	-2.9
Cougar Flat		2.1	1,937.8	5,750	-1.0
Tadpole Lake	w	2.1	1,939.9	5,340	-2.1
Elk Creek Trail 3510 and Winopee Lake Trail 16		0.4	1,940.3	5,263	-2.1
Snowshoe Lake Trail 33	w	1.2	1,941.5	5,254	-0.1
South end of Mink Lake Trail 3526	w	0.4	1,941.9	5,160	-2.6

Oregon

OREGON

Landmark	Facilities	Diff	S→N	Elev	Gra
Spur trail to Moody Lake	w: 0.20 m N	1.5	1,943.4	5,040	-0.9
Porky Lake Trail 4338		0.8	1,944.2	5,152	1.5
Climb gently to a seasonal creek		0.8	1,945.0	5,225	1.0
North end of Mink Lake Trail 3526 and Six Lakes Trail 14		0.7	1,945.7	5,354	2.0
Island Lake	w	0.8	1,946.5	5,443	1.2
Dumbbell Lake	w	0.7	1,947.2	5,527	1.3
Red Hill Trail 3515		2.1	1,949.3	5,496	-0.2
Sunset Lake Trail 3515.1		2.0	1,951.3	5,284	-1.2
Island Meadow Trail 3 to Elk Lake		1.3	1,952.6	5,250	-0.3
Elk Lake Resort Attn: (Your Name) PCT Hiker 60000 Century Dr. Bend, OR 97701 541-480-7378 Via UPS or FedEx only! $5 fee	w, G, M ,L, sh, R: 1.10 m E	0.0	1,952.6	5,250	-0.3
Horse Lake Trail		1.3	1,953.9	5,300	0.4
Camelot Lake	w	4.7	1,958.6	6,002	1.6
Sisters Mirror Lake	w	0.2	1,958.8	6,003	0.1
Nash Lake Trail 3527 and Mirror Lake Trail 20		0.2	1,959.0	5,989	-0.8
Wickiup Plain Trail		0.3	1,959.3	6,017	1.0
Broad county-line divide		1.2	1,960.5	6,218	1.8
Le Conte Crater Trail and side trail to Wickiup Plain Trail		0.4	1,960.9	6,160	-1.6
Descend to a creek	w	1.2	1,962.1	6,010	-1.4
North Fork of Mesa Creek	w	0.8	1,962.9	5,700	-4.2
James Creek Trail 3546		0.6	1,963.5	5,922	4.0
Cross Hinton Creek	w	2.2	1,965.7	6,282	1.8
Cross Separation Creek		0.5	1,966.2	6,400	2.6
Clear Reese Lake	w	0.3	1,966.5	6,460	2.2
Foley Ridge Trail 3511		1.4	1,967.9	6,294	-1.3

Oregon

OREGON

Landmark	Facilities	Diff	S→N	Elev	Gra
Linton Meadows Trail 3547		1.6	1,969.5	6,461	1.1
Obsidian Area		2.0	1,971.5	6,536	0.4
Obsidian Trail 3528	w	0.3	1,971.8	6,469	-2.4
Sister Spring	w	0.3	1,972.1	6,634	6.0
Glacier Way Trail 4336		0.9	1,973.0	6,399	-2.8
White Branch		1.9	1,974.9	6,512	0.6
Opie Dilldock Pass		0.6	1,975.5	6,900	7.0
Minnie Scott Spring	w	0.7	1,976.2	6,681	-3.4
Scott Trail 3551		1.0	1,977.2	6,277	-4.4
South Matthieu Lake	w	2.5	1,979.7	6,023	-1.1
South junction with North Matthieu Lake Trail 4062 (alternate route)		0.1	1,979.8	6,050	2.9
North junction with North Matthieu Lake Trail 4062 (end of alternate route)		2.1	1,981.9	5,455	-3.1
Trail to Lava Camp Lake, junction to a large trailhead parking area	w: 0.25 m NE	0.7	1,982.6	5,287	-2.6
Water Alert (↓): 16.4 m					
McKenzie Highway (OR 242)	R	1.2	1,983.8	5,309	0.2
General Delivery Sisters, OR 97759 541-549-0412	PO, w, G, M, L, sh, R: 15.00 m NE	0.0	1,983.8	5,309	0.2
Small trailhead parking area for OR 242 McKenzie Pass	R	0.3	1,984.1	5,210	-3.6
Little Belknap Trail 3003 to summit of Little Belknap		2.2	1,986.3	6,112	4.5
Trail switchbacks west-northwest		2.7	1,989.0	5,310	-3.2
Washington Ponds spur trail, very difficult to find		2.3	1,991.3	5,719	1.9
Coldwater Spring		2.4	1,993.7	5,200	-2.3
Unmarked climbers' trail to Washington Peak		0.5	1,994.2	5,050	-3.3
Descend north to fork with broad trail		0.9	1,995.1	4,775	-3.3

Oregon

OREGON

Landmark	Facilities	Diff	S→N	Elev	Gra
Big Lake Youth Camp Attn: (Your Name) PCT Hiker 26435 Big Lake Road Sisters, OR 97759 503-850-3562	w, M, sh, R: 0.70 m N	0.0	1,995.1	4,775	-3.3
Old Santiam Wagon Road	R	2.0	1,997.1	4,686	-0.5
Water Alert (↑): 16.7 m					
Lily-pad pond	w	1.9	1,999.0	4,796	0.6
Cross Santiam Highway (US 20)	R	1.9	2,000.9	4,804	0.0
Enter Mount Jefferson Wilderness		0.4	2,001.3	4,959	4.2
Santiam Lake Trail 3491		1.0	2,002.3	5,200	2.6
Curve north-northwest		2.5	2,004.8	6,000	3.5
Round Three Fingered Jack's northwest spur		2.6	2,007.4	6,390	1.6
Saddle along the Cascade divide		0.6	2,008.0	6,500	2.0
Minto Pass Trail 3437 south to Wasco Lake	w: 0.25 m S	3.2	2,011.2	5,350	-3.9
Old Summit Trail 4014	w: 0.50 m SE	0.5	2,011.7	5,430	1.7
Southeast spur of Peak 6,488		2.0	2,013.7	6,210	4.2
Rockpile Lake	w	1.1	2,014.8	6,274	0.6
Brush Creek Trail		0.4	2,015.2	6,140	-3.6
Swallow Lake Trail 3488		0.9	2,016.1	6,300	1.9
Reach a saddle		1.9	2,018.0	6,382	0.5
Small grassy meadow		1.4	2,019.4	6,240	-1.1
Escarpment where Mount Jefferson towers above		0.4	2,019.8	6,340	2.7
Unsigned trail climbs back to divide		0.7	2,020.5	6,130	-3.3
South end of Hunts Creek Trail 3440 (start of Pamelia Lake alternate route), reach a saddle		0.5	2,021.0	5,890	-5.2
West shore of placid Shale Lake	w	1.7	2,022.7	5,884	0.0
North end of Hunts Creek Trail 3440 (end of Pamelia Lake alternate route)		4.8	2,027.5	4,315	-3.5

Oregon

OREGON

Landmark	Facilities	Diff	S→N	Elev	Gra
Cross Milk Creek		0.2	2,027.7	4,320	0.3
Woodpecker Ridge Trail 3442		1.6	2,029.3	5,051	5.0
Jeff Creek	w	1.0	2,030.3	4,956	-1.0
Russell Creek	w	1.6	2,031.9	5,447	3.3
Whitewater Trail 3429		0.6	2,032.5	5,581	2.4
Ford Whitewater Creek	w	0.4	2,032.9	5,700	3.2
Spur to Scout Lake, reach Jefferson Park area		0.4	2,033.3	5,860	4.3
Spur trail to Scout and Bays Lakes		0.3	2,033.6	5,930	2.5
Junction with South Breitenbush Trail 3375		0.5	2,034.1	5,886	-1.0
Cross South Fork Breitenbush River		0.1	2,034.2	5,840	-5.0
Viewpoint		1.8	2,036.0	6,880	6.3
Leave Mount Jefferson Wilderness		3.0	2,039.0	5,591	-4.7
Spur road to FS 4220	w, R	0.4	2,039.4	5,515	-2.1
East shore of a shallow lake	w	0.6	2,040.0	5,750	4.3
Gibson Trail 708		1.0	2,041.0	5,552	-2.1
Horseshoe Saddle Trail 712		0.1	2,041.1	5,520	-3.5
Ruddy Hill Trail 714		0.3	2,041.4	5,600	2.9
Many Lakes Viewpoint		1.0	2,042.4	5,667	0.7
Upper Lake	w	0.8	2,043.2	5,384	-3.8
Cigar Lake	w	0.4	2,043.6	5,333	-1.4
Junction to Fork Lake		0.5	2,044.1	5,294	-0.8
Small triangular, semiclear lake	w	0.9	2,045.0	5,180	-1.5
Spur trail to Olallie Lake Resort	w	0.6	2,045.6	4,963	-3.4
Olallie Lake Resort	w, G, sh, R: 0.10 m E	0.0	2,045.6	4,963	-3.4
FS 4220, pass by Head Lake	w, R	0.1	2,045.7	4,969	0.7
Olallie Butte Trail 720		2.1	2,047.8	4,680	-1.5

OREGON

Landmark	Facilities	Diff	S→N	Elev	Gra
Lodgepole Trail 706		0.9	2,048.7	4,570	-1.3
Russ Lake Trail 716		0.4	2,049.1	4,606	1.0
Jude Lake	w	0.2	2,049.3	4,623	0.9
Lemiti Creek	w	5.3	2,054.6	4,362	-0.5
Junction to Trooper Springs	w: 0.05 m SW	0.4	2,055.0	4,394	0.9
Chinquapin Viewpoint		2.5	2,057.5	5,000	2.6
Cross a saddle		0.8	2,058.3	4,980	-0.3
Spur trail to a seeping spring	w: 0.05 m W	4.2	2,062.5	3,950	-2.7
Cross Warm Springs River	w	2.1	2,064.6	3,347	-3.1
Spur trail to another spring	w: 0.05 m SE	0.3	2,064.9	3,450	3.7
Junction with FS 4245	R	1.2	2,066.1	3,807	3.2
East slope of Summit Butte		1.7	2,067.8	4,230	2.7
Pass under high-voltage power line		0.3	2,068.1	4,210	-0.7
Unseen Red Wolf Pass		0.9	2,069.0	4,099	-1.3
Reach a jeep road	R	0.4	2,069.4	3,990	-3.0
Closed road FS S549	R	1.3	2,070.7	3,580	-3.4
Junction with Miller Trail 534 to Clackamas Lake Campground	w: 0.70 m NW	1.9	2,072.6	3,427	-0.9
Oak Grove Fork Clackamas River		0.6	2,073.2	3,350	-1.4
Skyline Road 42	R	0.2	2,073.4	3,370	1.1
Timothy Trail 528		1.3	2,074.7	3,286	-0.7
Crater Creek	w	3.8	2,078.5	3,234	-0.1
Little Crater Lake Trail 500	w: 0.12 m E	0.3	2,078.8	3,245	0.4
FS 5890	R	1.5	2,080.3	3,355	0.8
FS 58	R	1.6	2,081.9	3,879	3.6
FS 240	R	0.5	2,082.4	3,878	0.0
Seeping spring	w	0.3	2,082.7	3,928	1.8

Oregon

Landmark	Facilities	Diff	S→N	Elev	Gra
Climb north to a saddle		0.5	2,083.2	4,010	1.8
US 26 at Wapinitia Pass	R	3.3	2,086.5	3,914	-0.3
Switchback north to a near-crest junction to Twin Lakes Trail (alternate route)		1.4	2,087.9	4,397	3.7
Traverse north to a broad saddle		1.1	2,089.0	4,450	0.5
North end of Twin Lakes Trail (end of alternate route)		0.5	2,089.5	4,356	-2.0
Palmateer View Trail 482		0.5	2,090.0	4,450	2.0
Old section of OR 35 at Barlow Pass	R	1.5	2,091.5	4,157	-2.1
General Delivery Government Camp, OR 97028 503-272-3238	PO, w, G, R: 4.80 m W	0.0	2,091.5	4,157	-2.1
Cross new section of OR 35 near Barlow Pass	w, R: 0.10 m E	0.2	2,091.7	4,164	0.4
Ravine with usually flowing water	w	2.8	2,094.5	4,822	2.6
Join the Timberline Trail 600		1.1	2,095.6	5,345	5.2
White River Buried Forest Overlook		0.7	2,096.3	5,799	7.1
Cross upper Salmon River	w	0.4	2,096.7	5,982	5.0
Spur trail to Timberline Lodge		0.3	2,097.0	6,048	2.4
Timberline Lodge Guest Services Attn: (Your Name) PCT Hiker 27500 East Timberline Road Government Camp, OR 97028 503-272-3158 $10 fee	w, G, M, L, sh, r, R: 0.10 m S	0.0	2,097.0	6,048	2.4
Pass a radio tower		0.1	2,097.1	5,980	-7.4
Enter Mount Hood Wilderness		0.6	2,097.7	5,959	-0.4
Cross Little Zigzag River	w	0.3	2,098.0	5,832	-4.6
Hidden Lake Trail 779		0.4	2,098.4	5,715	-3.2
Cross silty Zigzag River	w	1.9	2,100.3	4,776	-5.4
South end of Paradise Park Loop Trail 757 (alternate route)		0.4	2,100.7	5,020	6.6
Paradise Park Trail 778		0.5	2,101.2	5,247	4.9

Oregon

OREGON

Landmark	Facilities	Diff	S→N	Elev	Gra
Lost Creek	w	0.8	2,102.0	5,375	1.7
Rushing Water Creek	w	0.6	2,102.6	5,480	1.9
North end of Paradise Park Loop Trail 757 (end of alternate route)		0.6	2,103.2	5,447	-0.6
Rushing Water Creek	w	3.1	2,106.3	3,388	-7.2
Flat bench		0.4	2,106.7	3,258	-3.5
South end of Ramona Falls Loop Trail 797– Timberline Trail 600 (alternate route)		0.2	2,106.9	3,323	3.5
Sandy River Trail 770		1.5	2,108.4	2,767	-4.0
Trail junction, about 70 yards before Muddy Fork		0.5	2,108.9	2,810	0.9
Ascend to a ridge		1.7	2,110.6	3,876	6.8
North end of Ramona Falls Loop Trail 797– Timberline Trail 600 (end of alternate route)		0.8	2,111.4	4,341	6.3
End of crestline before descending north		1.4	2,112.8	4,200	-1.1
Lolo Pass Road 18 at Lolo Pass	R	1.4	2,114.2	3,437	-5.9
Trickling creek	w	0.4	2,114.6	3,609	4.7
Junction with Huckleberry Mountain Trail 617	w: 0.30 m N	3.8	2,118.4	4,020	1.2
Spur trail to Salvation Spring Camp		0.2	2,118.6	4,085	3.5
Preachers Peak–Devils Pulpit saddle		0.7	2,119.3	4,340	4.0
Descend west to a notch		1.9	2,121.2	4,250	-0.5
Buck Peak Trail 615		0.6	2,121.8	4,491	4.4
Discover a small spring	w	0.3	2,122.1	4,426	-2.4
Reach the ridge again		0.3	2,122.4	4,230	-7.1
Reach abandoned FS 660	R	3.4	2,125.8	4,279	0.2
Spur of Indian Mountain with view of Mounts St. Helens, Rainier, and Adams		1.6	2,127.4	4,400	0.8
Indian Springs Campground	w	0.2	2,127.6	4,212	-10.0
Enter Mark O. Hatfield Wilderness		1.0	2,128.6	4,099	-1.2
South end of Eagle Creek Trail 440 to Wahtum Lake (alternate route)	w	1.7	2,130.3	3,751	-2.2

Oregon

OREGON

Landmark	Facilities	Diff	S→N	Elev	Gra
Lateral trail to Wahtum Lake Campground		0.3	2,130.6	3,778	1.0
Chinidere Mountain Trail		1.8	2,132.4	4,302	3.2
Saddle to a viewpoint		0.7	2,133.1	4,140	-2.5
Second saddle		1.4	2,134.5	3,830	-2.4
Camp Smokey saddle, third saddle		0.8	2,135.3	3,798	-0.4
Benson Way Trail 405B		0.4	2,135.7	4,070	7.4
Ruckel Creek Trail 405	w: 0.80 m W	0.9	2,136.6	4,097	0.3
Benson Ruckel Trail		0.8	2,137.4	3,930	-2.3
Second Benson Way Trail 405B		0.7	2,138.1	3,764	-2.6
Teakettle Spring	w	0.9	2,139.0	3,403	-4.4
Enter Columbia River Gorge National Scenic Area		2.4	2,141.4	1,753	-7.5
Junction to Columbia Gorge Work Center, lateral trail to Herman Creek		1.1	2,142.5	978	-7.7
Cross a creek	w	0.4	2,142.9	966	-0.3
Misnamed Dry Creek	w	1.9	2,144.8	705	-1.5
Power line road	R	0.8	2,145.6	698	-0.1
Southwest Undine Street (end of alternate route)		1.0	2,146.6	229	-5.1
General Delivery Cascade Locks, OR 97014 541-374-5026	PO, w, G, M, L, sh, r, R: 0.25 m NE	0.0	2,146.6	229	-5.1
Bridge of the Gods, east end	w	0.3	2,146.9	219	-0.4

PACIFIC CREST TRAIL: Washington

Vancouver

CANADA
UNITED STATES

E.C. Manning
Provincial Park

3

NORTH
CASCADES
NATIONAL
PARK

N49

20

20

97

Stehekin
2,571.8 mi.

5

MOUNT BAKER-
SNOQUALMIE
NATIONAL
FOREST

N48

OKANOGAN-
WENATCHEE
NATIONAL
FOREST

101

20

2

Stevens Pass/Skykomish
2,464.1 mi.

OLYMPIC
NATIONAL
PARK

Seattle

2

Wenatchee

90

Summit Inn
2,393.0 mi.

N47

90

Olympia

MOUNT RAINIER
NATIONAL
PARK

12

White Pass Post Office
2,294.9 mi.

GIFFORD
PINCHOT
NATIONAL
FOREST

395

82

97

N46

Trout Lake Grocery
2,228.9 mi.

26

5

Stevenson
2,147.2 mi.

WASHINGTON

OREGON

84

Cascade Locks
2,146.6 mi.

Portland

MOUNT HOOD
NATIONAL
FOREST

20 miles
20 kilometers

WASHINGTON

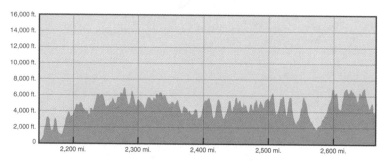

Elevation Profile for Washington
From the Oregon–Washington Border to Canada

SEGMENT TOTAL MILEAGE: 514.2 MILES

Landmark	Facilities	Diff	S→N	Elev	Gra
Bridge of the Gods, west end		0.3	2,147.2	192	-1.0
General Delivery Stevenson, WA 98648 509-427-5532	PO, w, G, M, L, sh, r, R: 2.70 m NE	0.0	2,147.2	192	-1.0
PCT trailhead		0.2	2,147.4	155	-2.0
Reach a spring	w, R	0.7	2,148.1	156	0.0
Cross a paved road	R	0.2	2,148.3	140	-0.9
Climb to a ridge, meet Tamanous Trail 27		0.4	2,148.7	372	6.3
Reach a utility road	R	1.8	2,150.5	420	0.3
Junction to Gillette Lake	w: 0.10 m E	0.3	2,150.8	311	-3.9
Bridge across Greenleaf Creek	w	0.9	2,151.7	482	2.1
Water Alert (↓): 14.4 m					
Low ridgecrest		1.9	2,153.6	1,107	3.6
Cross a road	R	0.5	2,154.1	1,411	6.6
Creeklet	R	0.6	2,154.7	1,707	5.4
Southwest up to a larger ridge		0.5	2,155.2	2,015	6.7

Washington

Landmark	Facilities	Diff	S→N	Elev	Gra
Viewpoint		1.3	2,156.5	2,480	3.9
Nearby road	R	0.7	2,157.2	2,761	4.4
Ridge above a power line saddle		0.5	2,157.7	3,120	7.8
Climb to a saddle and cross it, first view of Three Corner Rock		0.7	2,158.4	3,400	4.3
Leave Columbia River Gorge National Scenic Area		0.3	2,158.7	3,462	2.2
Crest-line road	R	1.2	2,159.9	3,025	-4.0
Spur trail to Three Corner Rock water trough, may have a leak	w: 0.30 m SW	2.2	2,162.1	3,255	1.1
Viewless saddle by CG 2090	R	1.4	2,163.5	2,343	-7.1
Crest gap		0.5	2,164.0	1,980	-7.9
CG 2000	R	1.6	2,165.6	1,737	-1.6
Water Alert (↑): 14.4 m					
Rock Creek	w	0.5	2,166.1	1,487	-5.4
Snag Creek	w	0.5	2,166.6	1,500	0.3
CG 2070	R	0.3	2,166.9	1,465	-1.3
Enter Gifford Pinchot National Forest		0.4	2,167.3	1,464	0.0
Seasonal creeklet	w	1.5	2,168.8	2,159	5.0
South-trending ridge		1.8	2,170.6	3,080	5.6
Second saddle, almost touch FS 41	R	0.7	2,171.3	2,985	-1.5
Cross abandoned FS 41	R	1.1	2,172.4	2,974	-0.1
Forest to main ridge		1.0	2,173.4	2,550	-4.6
Northeast down to a viewless saddle		0.7	2,174.1	2,150	-6.2
Cross a wide, splashing tributary of Trout Creek	w	2.3	2,176.4	1,301	-4.0
Cross FS 43 alongside Trout Creek	R	0.2	2,176.6	1,195	-5.8
Southeast to FS 417	R	0.8	2,177.4	1,156	-0.5
Bunker Hill Trail		0.6	2,178.0	1,216	1.1

Landmark	Facilities	Diff	S→N	Elev	Gra
Cross a crest		0.7	2,178.7	1,250	0.5
Little Soda Springs Road 54	R	0.7	2,179.4	966	-4.4
Cross Wind River	w	0.3	2,179.7	942	-0.9
Wind River Road	R	0.2	2,179.9	1,020	4.2
Cross FS 6517	R	0.9	2,180.8	1,191	2.1
Down to Panther Creek Road 65	R	1.2	2,182.0	939	-2.3
Panther Creek	w	0.2	2,182.2	890	-2.7
Westernmost end of a ridge		2.1	2,184.3	2,100	6.3
Saddle where a good dirt road starts	R	1.4	2,185.7	2,248	1.1
FS 68	R	1.4	2,187.1	2,784	4.2
Descend to a broad, open saddle		1.7	2,188.8	3,214	2.7
Cedar Creek Trail 149A	w: 0.30 m S	1.3	2,190.1	3,577	3.0
Grassy Knoll Trail 146 (and Big Huckleberry Mountain Summit Trail just paces later)		1.0	2,191.1	4,000	4.6
Second saddle crossing		1.4	2,192.5	3,730	-2.1
Descend to a gully with a reliable spring	w	0.5	2,193.0	3,556	-3.8
Reach a viewless, broad saddle		1.6	2,194.6	3,246	-2.1
Head toward FS 6801	R	0.8	2,195.4	3,220	-0.4
FS 60, back of Crest Horse Camp	R	2.5	2,197.9	3,495	1.2
Duck pond named Sheep Lake	w	1.7	2,199.6	4,027	3.4
Green Lake	w	1.1	2,200.7	4,257	2.3
Indian Race Track Shortcut Trail 171A		0.4	2,201.1	4,238	-0.5
Switchback to a saddle		2.9	2,204.0	4,730	1.8
Outlet creek of Lake Sebago		1.0	2,205.0	4,640	-1.0
Blue Lake	w	0.2	2,205.2	4,634	-0.3
East Crater Trail 48	w	1.9	2,207.1	4,775	0.8
Meet Lemei Lake Trail 33A		0.1	2,207.2	4,730	-4.9

Landmark	Facilities	Diff	S→N	Elev	Gra
Bear Lake, Elk Lake Trail 176	w	1.0	2,208.2	4,791	0.7
Slope above east end of Deer Lake		0.4	2,208.6	4,830	1.1
Indian Heaven Trail 33		0.3	2,208.9	4,897	2.4
Placid Lake Trail 29		1.0	2,209.9	5,000	1.1
Second saddle		0.5	2,210.4	5,110	2.4
West end of Cultus Creek Trail 108		0.4	2,210.8	5,140	0.8
South end of Sawtooth Trail 107 (alternate route)		1.3	2,212.1	4,852	-2.4
North end of Sawtooth Trail 107 (end of alternate route)		1.4	2,213.5	4,591	-2.0
Cross FS 24	R	1.2	2,214.7	4,269	-2.9
Descend to a saddle		1.3	2,216.0	4,070	-1.7
FS 8851	R	2.5	2,218.5	3,921	-0.6
Outlet of Big Mosquito Lake	w	0.1	2,218.6	3,900	-2.3
Cross a dirt road	R	2.2	2,220.8	4,115	1.1
Steamboat Lake spur trail	w	0.5	2,221.3	4,014	-2.2
FS 88	R	2.1	2,223.4	3,482	-2.8
Trout Lake Creek	w	0.4	2,223.8	3,318	-4.5
FS 8810	R	1.9	2,225.7	4,146	4.7
Reach a crest		0.6	2,226.3	4,570	7.7
FS 23 and FS 8810, Mount Adams Wilderness trailhead	w, R	2.6	2,228.9	3,849	-3.0
Trout Lake Grocery Attn: (Your Name) PCT Hiker PO Box 132 Trout Lake, WA 98680 509-395-2777 Via USPS	w, G, M, L, R: 13.60 m SE	0.0	2,228.9	3,849	-3.0
FS 521	R	0.8	2,229.7	4,021	2.3
Swampy Creek	w	0.2	2,229.9	4,020	0.0
Mount Adams Wilderness boundary		0.2	2,230.1	4,181	17.8

Washington

Landmark	Facilities	Diff	S→N	Elev	Gra
Spring 100 yards past White Salmon River	w	2.4	2,232.5	4,820	2.9
Stagman Ridge Trail 12		2.6	2,235.1	5,812	4.1
Round the Mountain Trail 9		0.4	2,235.5	5,901	2.4
Traverse to a saddle, east of Burnt Rock		3.2	2,238.7	5,950	0.2
Sheep Lake	w	0.3	2,239.0	5,783	-6.1
Cross Riley Creek	w	0.1	2,239.1	5,764	-2.1
Mutton Creek	w	1.3	2,240.4	5,893	1.1
Cross Lewis River	w	1.3	2,241.7	6,065	1.4
Divide Camp Trail 112		0.4	2,242.1	6,021	-1.2
Killen Creek Trail 113		1.3	2,243.4	6,115	0.8
Cross Killen Creek	w	0.9	2,244.3	5,924	-2.3
Highline Trail 114		0.2	2,244.5	5,918	-0.3
Readily accessible second pond, first one better	w	0.4	2,244.9	5,812	-2.9
Muddy Meadows Trail 13 to junction with Highline Trail		2.1	2,247.0	5,237	-3.0
Cross Muddy Fork	w	1.6	2,248.6	4,745	-3.3
Wooden bridge	w	0.5	2,249.1	4,627	-2.6
Trailside Lava Spring	w	0.4	2,249.5	4,522	-2.8
FS 5603	R	1.5	2,251.0	4,758	1.7
FS 115	R	2.0	2,253.0	4,502	-1.4
Cross Midway Creek	w	0.3	2,253.3	4,575	2.6
Leave last pond in a series of eight	w	2.8	2,256.1	5,081	2.0
Enter Goat Rocks Wilderness		1.3	2,257.4	4,981	-0.8
Coleman Weedpatch Trail 121		0.6	2,258.0	5,223	4.4
Climb to a saddle		0.7	2,258.7	5,450	3.5
Prominent ridgecrest		0.7	2,259.4	5,600	2.3

WASHINGTON

Landmark	Facilities	Diff	S→N	Elev	Gra
Cross a trickling creek	W	1.3	2,260.7	5,153	-3.7
Walupt Lake Trail 101		3.4	2,264.6	4,964	-0.5
Headwaters of Walupt Creek	W	4.1	2,268.7	5,577	1.6
Sheep Lake near Nannie Ridge Trail 98	W	0.7	2,269.4	5,765	2.9
Crest saddle, enter Yakama Nation Reservation territory		1.5	2,270.9	6,079	2.3
Cispus Pass		0.8	2,271.7	6,474	5.4
Easternmost tributary of Cispus River	W	0.7	2,272.4	6,146	-5.1
Bypass Trail 86 to Bypass Camp	w: 0.60 m W	1.6	2,274.0	5,964	-1.2
Snowgrass Trail 96		1.0	2,275.0	6,404	4.8
Former site of Dana May Yelverton Shelter		1.3	2,276.3	7,015	5.1
South end of Old Snowy Trail (alternate route)		0.3	2,276.6	7,095	2.9
North end of Old Snowy Trail (end of alternate route)		0.4	2,277.0	7,095	0.0
Upper end of Coyote Trail 79		1.6	2,278.6	6,690	-2.7
Almost touches a crest saddle		2.5	2,281.1	5,566	-4.9
Saddle that holds Lutz Lake	W	1.2	2,282.3	5,081	-4.4
Tieton Pass, North Fork Tieton and Clear Fork Trails	w: 0.25 m E	1.1	2,283.4	4,778	-3.0
Cross east over the divide		1.5	2,284.9	4,930	1.1
Hidden Spring Trail 1117	w: 0.30 m E	1.8	2,286.7	5,556	3.8
Shoe Lake Trail 1119		0.9	2,287.6	6,104	6.6
Top a narrow ridge		1.2	2,288.8	6,620	4.7
Chairlift Trail		2.7	2,291.5	5,805	-3.3
Round Mountain Trail 1144		1.1	2,292.6	5,434	-3.7
Ginnette Lake	W	0.2	2,292.8	5,419	-0.8
WA 12 (Old WA 14) near White Pass	R	2.1	2,294.9	4,409	-5.2

Landmark	Facilities	Diff	S→N	Elev	Gra
White Pass Post Office (The Kracker Barrel Store) Attn: (Your Name) PCT Hiker 48851 US 12 Naches, WA 98937 509-672-3105 $5 fee	PO, w, G, M, sh, r, R: 0.70 m W	0.0	2,294.9	4,409	-5.2
WA 12 parking lot		0.2	2,295.1	4,415	0.3
Dark Meadows Trail 1107, enter William O. Douglas Wilderness		1.0	2,296.1	4,816	4.4
Pass Deer Lake		1.0	2,297.1	5,181	4.0
Sand Lake	w	0.6	2,297.7	5,311	2.4
Cortright Creek Trail 57		1.9	2,299.6	5,481	1.0
Beusch Lake	w	1.3	2,300.9	5,101	-3.2
Dumbbell Lake Trail 1156	w	0.5	2,301.4	5,136	0.8
Good picnic spot next to Pipe Lake	w	0.6	2,302.0	5,197	1.1
Cowlitz Pass		0.5	2,302.5	5,168	-0.6
Cowlitz Trail 44		0.2	2,302.7	5,128	-2.2
Snow Lake	w	2.1	2,304.8	4,940	-1.0
Pothole Trail 45		1.0	2,305.8	4,849	-1.0
Jug Lake Trail 43		1.1	2,306.9	4,665	-1.8
Bumping River	w	0.4	2,307.3	4,604	-1.7
Outlet of Fish Lake	w	1.3	2,308.6	4,101	-4.2
Reliable drinkable rill	w	2.7	2,311.3	5,042	3.8
Laughingwater Trail		1.6	2,312.9	5,712	4.5
Two Lakes Trail 990	w: 0.30 m SE	1.7	2,314.6	5,603	-0.7
American Ridge Trail 958		2.6	2,317.2	5,350	-1.1
Anderson Lake	w	1.3	2,318.5	5,369	0.2
Dewey Lake Trail 968	w	1.9	2,320.4	5,158	-1.2
Walk along Dewey Lake	w, R	0.4	2,320.8	5,146	-0.3
Naches Peak Loop Trail	R	1.2	2,322.0	5,830	6.2

Landmark	Facilities	Diff	S→N	Elev	Gra
Exit William O. Douglas Wilderness	R	1.3	2,323.3	5,479	-2.9
WA 410 at Chinook Pass	w, R: 0.33 m S	0.2	2,323.5	5,434	-2.4
Sheep Lake	w	2.2	2,325.7	5,760	1.6
Sourdough Gap		1.2	2,326.9	6,385	5.7
Silver Creek Trail 1192		2.1	2,329.0	5,885	-2.6
Obscure trail signed FOG CITY and GOLD HILL		1.0	2,330.0	5,921	0.4
South end of Basin Trail 987		0.5	2,330.5	6,195	6.0
Blue Bell Pass		0.4	2,330.9	6,390	5.3
Bullion Basin Trail 1156		0.8	2,331.7	6,125	-3.6
Scout Pass		1.5	2,333.2	6,530	2.9
North end of Basin Trail 987 to Basin Lake	w: 0.50 m SE	0.2	2,333.4	6,384	-7.9
Reliable Big Crow Basin Spring near Norse Peak Trail	w	0.7	2,334.1	6,237	-2.3
Goat Lake Trail 1161 at Barnard saddle		0.9	2,335.0	6,105	-1.6
Hayden Pass		0.3	2,335.3	6,150	1.6
Martinson Gap, Castle Mountain Trail 1188		1.7	2,337.0	5,744	-2.6
Arch Rock Way 1187		2.6	2,339.6	5,941	0.8
Raven Roost–Cougar Valley Trail 951		0.7	2,340.3	5,820	-1.9
Junction to a broad summit		0.5	2,340.8	5,920	2.2
Spur trail to Arch Rock Spring	w: 0.10 m NW	0.8	2,341.6	5,685	-3.2
Louisiana Saddle Trail 945A		1.5	2,343.1	5,191	-3.6
Rods Gap		1.1	2,344.2	4,820	-3.7
Maggie Way Trail 1186		2.0	2,346.2	4,856	0.2
Camp Ulrich at Government Meadow	w	0.8	2,347.0	4,770	-1.2
Cross jeep road next to parking area	R	0.2	2,347.2	4,795	1.4
Junction to road going northeast	R	1.0	2,348.2	4,866	0.8
Pyramid Peak Trail		0.4	2,348.6	5,012	4.0

WASHINGTON

Landmark	Facilities	Diff	S→N	Elev	Gra
Windy Gap		1.0	2,349.6	5,200	2.0
Spring	w, R	2.1	2,351.7	5,053	-0.8
Water Alert (↓): 23.4 m					
Cross an unpaved road	R	0.2	2,351.9	5,013	-2.2
Descend to another road	R	1.0	2,352.9	4,749	-2.9
Road-laced crest saddle	R	1.4	2,354.3	4,899	1.2
Cross FS 784	R	1.1	2,355.4	4,967	0.7
Little Bear Creek Trail		1.5	2,356.9	5,329	2.6
Manastash Ridge Trail		0.7	2,357.6	5,557	3.5
Blowout Mountain Trail 1318		0.8	2,358.4	5,251	-4.2
Cross two roads to a major saddle	R	3.0	2,361.4	4,380	-3.2
Tacoma Pass		2.7	2,364.1	3,455	-3.7
Sheets Pass		1.4	2,365.5	3,702	1.9
Seasonal creek, good to mid-August only on a wet year		0.3	2,365.8	3,740	1.4
Broad saddle		3.8	2,369.6	4,195	1.3
Low point of the pass		2.3	2,371.9	4,329	0.6
Cross weather station access road	R	2.0	2,373.9	3,924	-2.2
Water Alert (↑): 23.2 m					
Stampede Pass Road 54, junction to Lizard Lake	w, R: 0.20 m S	1.0	2,374.9	3,671	-2.7
Trail follows logging road to a hairpin	R	1.9	2,376.8	3,851	1.0
Dandy Pass		0.3	2,377.1	3,680	-6.2
Come to a creek	w	1.9	2,379.0	3,512	-1.0
Stirrup Creek	w	0.8	2,379.8	3,447	-0.9
Headwaters of Meadow Creek		2.2	2,382.0	3,670	1.1
West shore of Twilight Lake	w	1.4	2,383.4	3,582	-0.7
Mirror Lake	w	0.9	2,384.3	4,201	7.5

WASHINGTON

Landmark	Facilities	Diff	S→N	Elev	Gra
Mirror Lake Trail 1302		0.3	2,384.6	4,231	1.1
North end of Cold Creek Trail, PCT heads west		0.5	2,385.1	4,524	6.4
Descend to a perennial creek	w: 0.05 m W	2.6	2,387.7	3,896	-2.6
Olallie Creek	w	0.6	2,388.3	3,634	-4.7
Power line access road	R	0.8	2,389.1	3,364	-3.7
Lodge Lake	w: 0.05 m N	1.8	2,390.9	3,168	-1.2
Beaver Lake	w	0.8	2,391.7	3,480	4.2
Trailhead parking area south of I-90		1.1	2,392.8	3,019	-4.6
WA 906	R	0.2	2,393.0	3,000	-1.0
Chevron Gas Station Attn: (Your Name) PCT Hiker 521 WA 906 Snoqualmie Pass, WA 98068 425-434-6688 $5 fee	w, G, M, L, R: 0.30 m SE	0.0	2,393.0	3,000	-1.0
Summit Inn Attn: (Your Name) PCT Hiker 603 WA 906 PO Box 163 Snoqualmie Pass, WA 98068 425-434-6300 $15 fee + tax if not staying	w, G, M, L, r, R: 0.30 m SE	0.0	2,393.0	3,000	-1.0
I-90 at Snoqualmie Pass	R	0.1	2,393.1	3,018	2.0
Northbound trailhead parking lot north of I-90	R	0.2	2,393.3	3,016	-0.1
Enter Alpine Lakes Wilderness	R	1.8	2,395.1	3,853	5.1
Commonwealth Basin Trail 1033	w: 0.30 m N	0.5	2,395.6	3,786	-1.5
Cross east side of the crest		3.2	2,398.8	5,440	5.6
Crest saddle between Ridge and Gravel Lakes	w	1.5	2,400.3	5,280	-1.2
Forested saddle between Joe and Edds Lakes		2.2	2,402.5	4,935	-1.7
Huckleberry saddle		1.4	2,403.9	5,560	4.9
Needle Sight Gap		0.5	2,404.4	5,930	8.1
Chikamin Pass		2.5	2,406.9	5,651	-1.2

Washington

Landmark	Facilities	Diff	S→N	Elev	Gra
Mineral Creek Trail 1331, spur trail to Park Lakes	w	1.0	2,407.9	4,911	-8.1
Three Queens		0.8	2,408.7	5,350	6.0
Spectacle Lake Trail 1306		1.6	2,410.3	4,430	-6.3
Delate Creek	w	0.9	2,411.2	3,941	-5.9
Pete Lake Trail 1323		1.9	2,413.1	3,245	-4.0
Lemah Creek	w	0.7	2,413.8	3,198	-0.7
Lemah Meadow Trail 1323B	w	0.6	2,414.4	3,228	0.5
Switchback out of Lemah Creek		0.8	2,415.2	3,370	1.9
Secluded cirque with a chilly tarn	w	4.7	2,419.9	5,520	5.0
Cross an inlet	w	1.3	2,421.2	5,300	-1.8
Creek	w	1.3	2,422.5	5,255	-0.4
Waptus Burn Trail 1329C		0.4	2,422.9	5,171	-2.3
Dutch Miller Gap Trail 1030		4.8	2,427.7	3,045	-4.8
Waptus River	w	0.1	2,427.8	3,027	-2.0
Waptus River Trail 1310	w	0.8	2,428.6	3,111	1.1
Second stream near Spade Lake Trail 1337	w	1.4	2,430.0	3,234	1.0
Spinola Creek Trail 1310A		1.0	2,431.0	3,348	1.2
Lake Vicente Trail 1365		3.3	2,434.3	4,441	3.6
Deep Lake's access trail	w	0.5	2,434.8	4,379	-1.3
Peggys Pond Trail 1375		2.7	2,437.5	5,526	4.6
Cathedral Pass		0.2	2,437.7	5,610	4.6
Few small tarns		0.1	2,437.8	5,540	-7.6
Junction of two streams	w	2.0	2,439.8	4,589	-5.2
Cross second creek carefully, drains Mount Daniel's northeast slopes	w	1.3	2,441.1	3,806	-6.6
Cross headwaters of Cle Elum drainage where trail turns east	w	1.1	2,442.2	4,236	4.2
Deception Pass		0.6	2,442.8	4,478	4.4

Landmark	Facilities	Diff	S→N	Elev	Gra
Cross a stream	w	1.9	2,444.7	4,467	-0.1
Cross outlet of Deception Lakes	w	1.5	2,446.2	5,006	3.9
Pieper Pass		2.0	2,448.2	5,933	5.0
Glacier Lake	w	1.6	2,449.8	5,036	-6.1
Surprise Creek Trail 1060	w	0.8	2,450.6	4,863	-2.3
Trap Pass Trail 1060A		1.0	2,451.6	5,080	2.4
Trap Pass		0.9	2,452.5	5,623	6.6
Access trail to Trap Lake		0.2	2,452.7	5,350	-15.0
Seasonal creek	w	0.6	2,453.3	5,263	-1.6
Climb to a notch		0.7	2,454.0	5,210	-0.8
Hope Lake	w	1.9	2,455.9	4,385	-4.7
North end of Mig Lake	w	0.8	2,456.7	4,662	3.8
Unnamed crest saddle		1.8	2,458.5	5,190	3.2
Josephine Lake's cirque		0.8	2,459.3	4,940	-3.4
North shore of Lake Susan Jane	w	0.5	2,459.8	4,577	-7.9
Saddle near the top of a chairlift		2.2	2,462.0	5,160	2.9
US 2 at Stevens Pass, parking area	R	2.1	2,464.1	4,053	-5.7
Stevens Pass Attn: (Your Name) PCT Hiker 93001 US 2 Skykomish, WA 98288 206-812-4510 Via UPS or FedEx only! stevenspass.com for details	w, M, R: 0.10 m W	0.0	2,464.1	4,053	-5.7
General Delivery Skykomish, WA 98288 360-677-2241	PO, w, G, M, L, r, R: 14.00 m W	0.0	2,464.1	4,053	-5.7
3-yard-wide tributary of Nason Creek	w	2.5	2,466.6	3,881	-0.7
Enter Henry M. Jackson Wilderness		0.9	2,467.5	4,169	3.5
Meadow where Nason Creek flows	w	0.1	2,467.6	4,220	5.5
Switchback up to a saddle		2.0	2,469.6	5,030	4.4

WASHINGTON

Landmark	Facilities	Diff	S→N	Elev	Gra
Spur trail to Lake Valhalla	w	0.3	2,469.9	4,900	-4.7
Smithbrook Trail 1590		1.8	2,471.7	4,688	-1.3
Delightful cascade	w	1.8	2,473.5	4,200	-2.9
Lake Janus	w	0.4	2,473.9	4,146	-1.5
Reach a crest		1.6	2,475.5	5,180	7.0
Meadow with faint trail to Glasses Lake		0.8	2,476.3	5,070	-1.5
West shoulder of Grizzly Peak		2.3	2,478.6	5,580	2.4
Cross the crest above Grizzly Lake		1.4	2,480.0	5,120	-3.6
Wenatchee Pass		1.2	2,481.2	4,245	-7.9
Top Lake Trail 1506		0.7	2,481.9	4,581	5.2
Meadows Creek Trail 1057 to Pear Lake's cirque	w	0.6	2,482.5	4,860	5.1
Up to the crest		1.6	2,484.1	5,350	3.3
Fairly reliable creeks	w	2.6	2,486.7	4,777	-2.4
Saddle Gap		0.7	2,487.4	5,002	3.5
West Cady Ridge Trail 1054		0.3	2,487.7	4,930	-2.6
Pass Creek Trail 1053, next to 10-foot-wide Pass Creek	w	1.4	2,489.1	4,165	-5.9
Cady Pass, Cady Creek Trail 1501		0.5	2,489.6	4,303	3.0
Switchback to a crest		1.9	2,491.5	5,470	6.7
Lake Sally Ann	w	2.0	2,493.5	5,476	0.0
Cady Ridge Trail 1532		0.4	2,493.9	5,385	-2.5
Wards Pass		0.7	2,494.6	5,700	4.9
Bald Eagle Trail 650		0.6	2,495.2	5,600	-1.8
Spur trail to Little Wenatchee River Trail 1525		0.8	2,496.0	5,440	-2.2
Little Wenatchee River Trail 1525		0.2	2,496.2	5,496	3.0
Kodak Peak's east ridge		0.7	2,496.9	5,660	2.5
Indian Pass		1.3	2,498.2	4,973	-5.7

WASHINGTON

Landmark	Facilities	Diff	S→N	Elev	Gra
Kid Pond		1.0	2,499.2	5,320	3.8
Lower White Pass		0.6	2,499.8	5,411	1.6
Semiclear Reflection Pond	w	0.4	2,500.2	5,588	4.8
Junction at White Pass		1.8	2,502.0	5,904	1.9
North Fork Sauk Trail 649		0.5	2,502.5	6,011	2.3
Red Pass		1.3	2,503.8	6,488	4.0
Descend to a lone 3-foot-high cairn		1.4	2,505.2	5,700	-6.1
Some campsites		0.3	2,505.5	5,453	-9.0
Last crossing of a swelling creek	w	1.3	2,506.8	4,741	-6.0
Cross White Chuck River	w	0.9	2,507.7	4,076	-8.0
Baekos Creek	w	1.0	2,508.7	3,944	-1.4
Chetwot Creek	w	1.3	2,510.0	3,741	-1.7
Sitkum Creek	w	1.4	2,511.4	4,150	3.2
Kennedy Creek	w	0.9	2,512.3	3,942	-2.5
Kennedy Ridge Trail 639		0.4	2,512.7	4,168	6.1
Glacier Creek	w	1.8	2,514.5	5,300	6.8
Glacier Ridge Trail 658		0.7	2,515.2	5,728	6.6
Cross Pumice Creek	w	0.5	2,515.7	5,684	-1.0
Contour over to a ridge		1.6	2,517.3	5,669	-0.1
Cross Fire Creek	w	0.5	2,517.8	5,279	-8.5
Fire Creek Pass		2.4	2,520.2	5,820	2.4
Outlet of Mica Lake	w	0.6	2,520.8	5,455	-6.6
Small bench, next to Mica Creek	w	0.5	2,521.3	5,161	-6.4
Reach another creek	w	1.5	2,522.8	4,400	-5.5
Milk Creek Trail 790 (not an exit route; bridge out)		2.0	2,524.8	3,289	-6.0
Reach a ridgecrest		4.5	2,529.3	5,950	6.4

Landmark	Facilities	Diff	S→N	Elev	Gra
Small knoll		1.0	2,530.3	5,860	-1.0
Grassy Point Trail 788		0.6	2,530.9	6,100	4.3
Dolly Vista campsite		0.6	2,531.5	5,724	-6.8
Saddle on Vista Ridge		0.5	2,532.0	5,380	-7.5
Reach Vista Creek	w	3.2	2,535.2	3,619	-6.0
Vista Creek (do not cross)		2.3	2,537.5	2,884	-3.5
Dolly Creek	w	2.5	2,540.0	2,409	-2.1
Suiattle River Bridge	w	0.6	2,540.6	2,318	-1.6
East-west Suiattle River Trail 784, go east		0.3	2,540.9	2,508	6.9
Miners Ridge Trail 785		2.4	2,543.3	2,819	1.4
First crossing of Miners Creek		1.1	2,544.4	2,752	-0.7
Buck Creek Pass Trail		4.2	2,548.6	4,628	4.9
Second crossing of Miners Creek	w	0.6	2,549.2	4,483	-2.6
Miners Cabin Trail 795		1.8	2,551.0	5,486	6.1
Cloudy Pass Trail		0.8	2,551.8	5,906	5.7
Suiattle Pass		0.2	2,552.0	5,990	4.6
Down to a creeklet	w	0.4	2,552.4	5,806	-5.0
First downhill to a canyon with campsite		1.5	2,553.9	5,056	-5.4
Spur trail to signed campsite	w	1.6	2,555.5	5,377	2.2
Spur trail to some tent sites	w	1.6	2,557.1	4,724	-4.4
Hemlock Camp	w	2.4	2,559.5	3,552	-5.3
Spruce Creek Camp	w	2.8	2,562.3	2,876	-2.6
Swamp Creek Camp	w	1.5	2,563.8	2,749	-0.9
Near South Fork Agnes Creek		1.6	2,565.4	2,570	-1.2
West Fork Agnes Creek Trail 1272, Five Mile Camp	w	1.4	2,566.8	2,206	-2.8
Seasonal Trapper Creek		1.1	2,567.9	2,120	-0.8

Landmark	Facilities	Diff	S→N	Elev	Gra
Agnes Creek	w	3.7	2,571.6	1,560	-1.6
Stehekin Valley Road	R	0.2	2,571.8	1,662	5.5
General Delivery Stehekin, WA 98852 509-682-2625	PO, w, G, M, L, sh, r, R: 10.60 m E	0.0	2,571.8	1,662	5.5
High Bridge Ranger Station		0.1	2,571.9	1,611	-5.5
Junction to Cascade Corral		0.4	2,572.3	1,851	6.5
Howard Lake	w	0.9	2,573.2	2,180	4.0
Old Wagon Trail		0.8	2,574.0	1,940	-3.3
McGregor Creek	w	0.4	2,574.4	2,204	7.2
Buzzard Creek	w	0.5	2,574.9	2,244	0.9
Canim Creek	w	0.6	2,575.5	2,160	-1.5
Bridge Creek Ranger Station	w	1.3	2,576.8	2,101	-0.5
PCT Bridge Creek trailhead on Stehekin River road	R	0.3	2,577.1	2,180	2.9
Cross Berry Creek	w	1.6	2,578.7	2,708	3.6
Bridge Creek	w	1.0	2,579.7	2,540	-1.8
North Fork Bridge Creek Trail 1233		0.3	2,580.0	2,815	10.0
Maple Creek	w	1.6	2,581.6	3,097	1.9
Spur trail to Six Mile Camp	w: 0.13 m SE	1.5	2,583.1	3,134	0.3
Rainbow Lake Trail		0.7	2,583.8	3,258	1.9
Spur trail to Bridge Creek	w: 0.10 m SW	1.5	2,585.3	3,512	1.8
Twisp Pass Trail 432		0.9	2,586.2	3,632	1.4
Southeast flank of Frisco Mountain		0.8	2,587.0	3,855	3.0
Bridge Creek		1.7	2,588.7	4,303	2.9
Spur trail to WA 20 parking lot		0.9	2,589.6	4,514	2.5
Rainy Lake's outlet creek	w	0.7	2,590.3	4,712	3.1
Rainy Pass picnic area	R	0.8	2,591.1	4,855	1.9

Washington

Landmark	Facilities	Diff	S→N	Elev	Gra
North end of parking lot after crossing WA 20	R	0.3	2,591.4	4,882	1.0
Porcupine Creek	w	1.7	2,593.1	5,299	2.7
Pass some campsites		1.8	2,594.9	6,155	5.2
Cutthroat Pass		1.5	2,596.4	6,837	4.9
Granite Pass		2.4	2,598.8	6,263	-2.6
Large campsite	w	2.1	2,600.9	6,241	-0.1
Methow Pass		0.9	2,601.8	6,593	4.2
Golden Creek	w	4.1	2,605.9	4,584	-5.3
West Fork Methow River and campsite	w	0.7	2,606.6	4,384	-3.1
Merge with East Creek Trail 756		0.8	2,607.4	4,380	-0.1
Mill Creek Trail 755		0.2	2,607.6	4,380	0.0
West Fork Methow Trail 480, next to Brush Creek	w	1.9	2,609.5	4,305	-0.4
Water Alert (↓): 12.9 m					
Glacier Pass		2.7	2,612.2	5,581	5.1
Alpine-garden pass above South Fork Trout Creek		2.6	2,614.8	6,866	5.4
Relaxing spot		1.3	2,616.1	6,600	-2.2
Windy, scenic pass on southwest shoulder of Tatie Peak		0.9	2,617.0	6,900	3.6
20 yards before FS 500	R	2.8	2,619.8	6,550	-1.4
Minor gap		0.9	2,620.7	6,363	-2.3
Harts Pass		1.3	2,622.0	6,188	-1.5
Water Alert (↑): 12.9 m					
Seasonal stream	w	0.4	2,622.4	6,365	4.8
Junction with a spur trail to a U.S. Forest Service road	R	1.0	2,623.4	6,852	5.3
Pass above Benson Creek		2.2	2,625.6	6,700	-0.7
Buffalo Pass		0.7	2,626.3	6,557	-2.2

WASHINGTON

Landmark	Facilities	Diff	S→N	Elev	Gra
Windy Pass		0.9	2,627.2	6,273	-3.4
Seasonal stream at the foot of Tamarack Peak	w	0.6	2,627.8	6,512	4.3
Foggy Pass		1.6	2,629.4	6,182	-2.2
Jim Pass		0.7	2,630.1	6,265	1.3
Devils Backbone		1.3	2,631.4	6,180	-0.7
Shaw Creek	w	0.8	2,632.2	5,801	-5.1
Holman Pass		3.3	2,635.5	5,066	-2.4
Goat Lakes Creek	w	1.3	2,636.8	5,560	4.1
Spring	w	1.1	2,637.9	6,200	6.3
Rock Pass		1.1	2,639.0	6,502	3.0
Rock Creek Trail 473		2.1	2,641.1	6,353	-0.8
Misnamed Woody Pass		0.5	2,641.6	6,624	5.9
Unnamed summit on Lakeview Ridge		3.2	2,644.8	7,126	1.7
Spur trail to Hopkins Lake, campsites	w	1.4	2,646.2	6,254	-6.8
Hopkins Pass		0.3	2,646.5	6,140	-4.1
Castle Pass		2.4	2,648.9	5,460	-3.1
Monument 78, United States–Canada border, close to Castle Creek		3.7	2,652.6	4,258	-3.5
Castle Creek	w	0.3	2,652.9	4,215	-1.6
Southwest base of Windy Joe Mountain		3.5	2,656.4	5,035	2.5
Frosty Mountain Trail		0.1	2,656.5	5,110	8.2
Windy Joe Trail	R	1.0	2,657.5	5,220	1.2
Junction with old PCT route		1.8	2,659.3	4,100	-6.8
Little Muddy Creek		0.9	2,660.2	3,855	-3.0
Trailhead parking area with MANNING PARK sign		1.2	2,661.4	3,910	0.5
Lightning Lake Campground Reservation only 800-689-9025	w, R: 2.00 m W	0.0	2,661.4	3,910	0.5

WASHINGTON

Landmark	Facilities	Diff	S→N	Elev	Gra
Manning Park Resort 250-840-8822	w, G, M, L, R: 0.67 m E	0.0	2,661.4	3,910	0.5
Manning Park Headquarters BC, Canada V0X 1R0	w, r, R: 0.87 m E	0.0	2,661.4	3,910	0.5
Coldspring Campground 50% reservation only 800-689-9025, go toward Manning Park Resort first east, and then west	w, R: 1.90 m NW	0.0	2,661.4	3,910	0.5

CALENDAR

2022

January

Sun	Mon	Tue	Wed	Thu	Fri	Sat
						1
2	3	4	5	6	7	8
9	10	11	12	13	14	15
16	17	18	19	20	21	22
23	24	25	26	27	28	29
30	31					

February

Sun	Mon	Tue	Wed	Thu	Fri	Sat
		1	2	3	4	5
6	7	8	9	10	11	12
13	14	15	16	17	18	19
20	21	22	23	24	25	26
27	28					

March

Sun	Mon	Tue	Wed	Thu	Fri	Sat
		1	2	3	4	5
6	7	8	9	10	11	12
13	14	15	16	17	18	19
20	21	22	23	24	25	26
27	28	29	30	31		

April

Sun	Mon	Tue	Wed	Thu	Fri	Sat
					1	2
3	4	5	6	7	8	9
10	11	12	13	14	15	16
17	18	19	20	21	22	23
24	25	26	27	28	29	30

May

Sun	Mon	Tue	Wed	Thu	Fri	Sat
1	2	3	4	5	6	7
8	9	10	11	12	13	14
15	16	17	18	19	20	21
22	23	24	25	26	27	28
29	30	31				

June

Sun	Mon	Tue	Wed	Thu	Fri	Sat
			1	2	3	4
5	6	7	8	9	10	11
12	13	14	15	16	17	18
19	20	21	22	23	24	25
26	27	28	29	30		

July

Sun	Mon	Tue	Wed	Thu	Fri	Sat
					1	2
3	4	5	6	7	8	9
10	11	12	13	14	15	16
17	18	19	20	21	22	23
24	25	26	27	28	29	30
31						

August

Sun	Mon	Tue	Wed	Thu	Fri	Sat
	1	2	3	4	5	6
7	8	9	10	11	12	13
14	15	16	17	18	19	20
21	22	23	24	25	26	27
28	29	30	31			

September

Sun	Mon	Tue	Wed	Thu	Fri	Sat
				1	2	3
4	5	6	7	8	9	10
11	12	13	14	15	16	17
18	19	20	21	22	23	24
25	26	27	28	29	30	

October

Sun	Mon	Tue	Wed	Thu	Fri	Sat
						1
2	3	4	5	6	7	8
9	10	11	12	13	14	15
16	17	18	19	20	21	22
23	24	25	26	27	28	29
30	31					

November

Sun	Mon	Tue	Wed	Thu	Fri	Sat
		1	2	3	4	5
6	7	8	9	10	11	12
13	14	15	16	17	18	19
20	21	22	23	24	25	26
27	28	29	30			

December

Sun	Mon	Tue	Wed	Thu	Fri	Sat
				1	2	3
4	5	6	7	8	9	10
11	12	13	14	15	16	17
18	19	20	21	22	23	24
25	26	27	28	29	30	31

Post Office Holidays

Jan. 1, Jan. 17, Feb. 21, May 30, July 4,

Sept. 5, Oct. 10, Nov. 11, Nov. 24, Dec. 26

CALENDAR

2023

January

Sun	Mon	Tue	Wed	Thu	Fri	Sat
1	2	3	4	5	6	7
8	9	10	11	12	13	14
15	16	17	18	19	20	21
22	23	24	25	26	27	28
29	30	31				

February

Sun	Mon	Tue	Wed	Thu	Fri	Sat
			1	2	3	4
5	6	7	8	9	10	11
12	13	14	15	16	17	18
19	20	21	22	23	24	25
26	27	28				

March

Sun	Mon	Tue	Wed	Thu	Fri	Sat
			1	2	3	4
5	6	7	8	9	10	11
12	13	14	15	16	17	18
19	20	21	22	23	24	25
26	27	28	29	30	31	

April

Sun	Mon	Tue	Wed	Thu	Fri	Sat
						1
2	3	4	5	6	7	8
9	10	11	12	13	14	15
16	17	18	19	20	21	22
23	24	25	26	27	28	29
30						

May

Sun	Mon	Tue	Wed	Thu	Fri	Sat
	1	2	3	4	5	6
7	8	9	10	11	12	13
14	15	16	17	18	19	20
21	22	23	24	25	26	27
28	29	30	31			

June

Sun	Mon	Tue	Wed	Thu	Fri	Sat
				1	2	3
4	5	6	7	8	9	10
11	12	13	14	15	16	17
18	19	20	21	22	23	24
25	26	27	28	29	30	

July

Sun	Mon	Tue	Wed	Thu	Fri	Sat
						1
2	3	4	5	6	7	8
9	10	11	12	13	14	15
16	17	18	19	20	21	22
23	24	25	26	27	28	29
30	31					

August

Sun	Mon	Tue	Wed	Thu	Fri	Sat
		1	2	3	4	5
6	7	8	9	10	11	12
13	14	15	16	17	18	19
20	21	22	23	24	25	26
27	28	29	30	31		

September

Sun	Mon	Tue	Wed	Thu	Fri	Sat
					1	2
3	4	5	6	7	8	9
10	11	12	13	14	15	16
17	18	19	20	21	22	23
24	25	26	27	28	29	30

October

Sun	Mon	Tue	Wed	Thu	Fri	Sat
1	2	3	4	5	6	7
8	9	10	11	12	13	14
15	16	17	18	19	20	21
22	23	24	25	26	27	28
29	30	31				

November

Sun	Mon	Tue	Wed	Thu	Fri	Sat
			1	2	3	4
5	6	7	8	9	10	11
12	13	14	15	16	17	18
19	20	21	22	23	24	25
26	27	28	29	30		

December

Sun	Mon	Tue	Wed	Thu	Fri	Sat
					1	2
3	4	5	6	7	8	9
10	11	12	13	14	15	16
17	18	19	20	21	22	23
24	25	26	27	28	29	30
31						

Post Office Holidays

Jan. 2, Jan. 16, Feb. 20, May 29, July 4,

Sept. 4, Oct. 9, Nov. 10, Nov. 23, Dec. 25

CALENDAR

2024

January

Sun	Mon	Tue	Wed	Thu	Fri	Sat
	1	2	3	4	5	6
7	8	9	10	11	12	13
14	15	16	17	18	19	20
21	22	23	24	25	26	27
28	29	30	31			

February

Sun	Mon	Tue	Wed	Thu	Fri	Sat
				1	2	3
4	5	6	7	8	9	10
11	12	13	14	15	16	17
18	19	20	21	22	23	24
25	26	27	28	29		

March

Sun	Mon	Tue	Wed	Thu	Fri	Sat
					1	2
3	4	5	6	7	8	9
10	11	12	13	14	15	16
17	18	19	20	21	22	23
24	25	26	27	28	29	30
31						

April

Sun	Mon	Tue	Wed	Thu	Fri	Sat
	1	2	3	4	5	6
7	8	9	10	11	12	13
14	15	16	17	18	19	20
21	22	23	24	25	26	27
28	29	30				

May

Sun	Mon	Tue	Wed	Thu	Fri	Sat
			1	2	3	4
5	6	7	8	9	10	11
12	13	14	15	16	17	18
19	20	21	22	23	24	25
26	27	28	29	30	31	

June

Sun	Mon	Tue	Wed	Thu	Fri	Sat
						1
2	3	4	5	6	7	8
9	10	11	12	13	14	15
16	17	18	19	20	21	22
23	24	25	26	27	28	29
30						

July

Sun	Mon	Tue	Wed	Thu	Fri	Sat
	1	2	3	4	5	6
7	8	9	10	11	12	13
14	15	16	17	18	19	20
21	22	23	24	25	26	27
28	29	30	31			

August

Sun	Mon	Tue	Wed	Thu	Fri	Sat
				1	2	3
4	5	6	7	8	9	10
11	12	13	14	15	16	17
18	19	20	21	22	23	24
25	26	27	28	29	30	31

September

Sun	Mon	Tue	Wed	Thu	Fri	Sat
1	2	3	4	5	6	7
8	9	10	11	12	13	14
15	16	17	18	19	20	21
22	23	24	25	26	27	28
29	30					

October

Sun	Mon	Tue	Wed	Thu	Fri	Sat
		1	2	3	4	5
6	7	8	9	10	11	12
13	14	15	16	17	18	19
20	21	22	23	24	25	26
27	28	29	30	31		

November

Sun	Mon	Tue	Wed	Thu	Fri	Sat
					1	2
3	4	5	6	7	8	9
10	11	12	13	14	15	16
17	18	19	20	21	22	23
24	25	26	27	28	29	30

December

Sun	Mon	Tue	Wed	Thu	Fri	Sat
1	2	3	4	5	6	7
8	9	10	11	12	13	14
15	16	17	18	19	20	21
22	23	24	25	26	27	28
29	30	31				

Post Office Holidays

Jan. 1, Jan. 15, Feb. 19, May 27, July 4,

Sept. 2, Oct. 14, Nov. 11, Nov. 28, Dec. 25

CALENDAR

2025

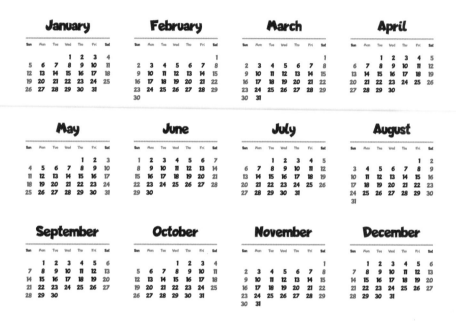

January

Sun	Mon	Tue	Wed	Thu	Fri	Sat
			1	2	3	4
5	6	7	8	9	10	11
12	13	14	15	16	17	18
19	20	21	22	23	24	25
26	27	28	29	30	31	

February

Sun	Mon	Tue	Wed	Thu	Fri	Sat
						1
2	3	4	5	6	7	8
9	10	11	12	13	14	15
16	17	18	19	20	21	22
23	24	25	26	27	28	29
30						

March

Sun	Mon	Tue	Wed	Thu	Fri	Sat
						1
2	3	4	5	6	7	8
9	10	11	12	13	14	15
16	17	18	19	20	21	22
23	24	25	26	27	28	29
30	31					

April

Sun	Mon	Tue	Wed	Thu	Fri	Sat
		1	2	3	4	5
6	7	8	9	10	11	12
13	14	15	16	17	18	19
20	21	22	23	24	25	26
27	28	29	30			

May

Sun	Mon	Tue	Wed	Thu	Fri	Sat
				1	2	3
4	5	6	7	8	9	10
11	12	13	14	15	16	17
18	19	20	21	22	23	24
25	26	27	28	29	30	31

June

Sun	Mon	Tue	Wed	Thu	Fri	Sat
1	2	3	4	5	6	7
8	9	10	11	12	13	14
15	16	17	18	19	20	21
22	23	24	25	26	27	28
29	30					

July

Sun	Mon	Tue	Wed	Thu	Fri	Sat
		1	2	3	4	5
6	7	8	9	10	11	12
13	14	15	16	17	18	19
20	21	22	23	24	25	26
27	28	29	30	31		

August

Sun	Mon	Tue	Wed	Thu	Fri	Sat
					1	2
3	4	5	6	7	8	9
10	11	12	13	14	15	16
17	18	19	20	21	22	23
24	25	26	27	28	29	30
31						

September

Sun	Mon	Tue	Wed	Thu	Fri	Sat
	1	2	3	4	5	6
7	8	9	10	11	12	13
14	15	16	17	18	19	20
21	22	23	24	25	26	27
28	29	30				

October

Sun	Mon	Tue	Wed	Thu	Fri	Sat
			1	2	3	4
5	6	7	8	9	10	11
12	13	14	15	16	17	18
19	20	21	22	23	24	25
26	27	28	29	30	31	

November

Sun	Mon	Tue	Wed	Thu	Fri	Sat
						1
2	3	4	5	6	7	8
9	10	11	12	13	14	15
16	17	18	19	20	21	22
23	24	25	26	27	28	29
30	31					

December

Sun	Mon	Tue	Wed	Thu	Fri	Sat
	1	2	3	4	5	6
7	8	9	10	11	12	13
14	15	16	17	18	19	20
21	22	23	24	25	26	27
28	29	30	31			

Post Office Holidays

Jan. 1, Jan. 20, Feb. 17, May 28, July 4,

Sept. 1, Oct. 13, Nov. 11, Nov. 27, Dec. 25

CALENDAR

2026

January

Sun	Mon	Tue	Wed	Thu	Fri	Sat
				1	2	3
4	5	6	7	8	9	10
11	12	13	14	15	16	17
18	19	20	21	22	23	24
25	26	27	28	29	30	31

February

Sun	Mon	Tue	Wed	Thu	Fri	Sat
1	2	3	4	5	6	7
8	9	10	11	12	13	14
15	16	17	18	19	20	21
22	23	24	25	26	27	28

March

Sun	Mon	Tue	Wed	Thu	Fri	Sat
1	2	3	4	5	6	7
8	9	10	11	12	13	14
15	16	17	18	19	20	21
22	23	24	25	26	27	28
29	30	31				

April

Sun	Mon	Tue	Wed	Thu	Fri	Sat
			1	2	3	4
5	6	7	8	9	10	11
12	13	14	15	16	17	18
19	20	21	22	23	24	25
26	27	28	29	30		

May

Sun	Mon	Tue	Wed	Thu	Fri	Sat
					1	2
3	4	5	6	7	8	9
10	11	12	13	14	15	16
17	18	19	20	21	22	23
24	25	26	27	28	29	30
31						

June

Sun	Mon	Tue	Wed	Thu	Fri	Sat
	1	2	3	4	5	6
7	8	9	10	11	12	13
14	15	16	17	18	19	20
21	22	23	24	25	26	27
28	29	30				

July

Sun	Mon	Tue	Wed	Thu	Fri	Sat
			1	2	3	4
5	6	7	8	9	10	11
12	13	14	15	16	17	18
19	20	21	22	23	24	25
26	27	28	29	30	31	

August

Sun	Mon	Tue	Wed	Thu	Fri	Sat
						1
2	3	4	5	6	7	8
9	10	11	12	13	14	15
16	17	18	19	20	21	22
23	24	25	26	27	28	29
30	31					

September

Sun	Mon	Tue	Wed	Thu	Fri	Sat
		1	2	3	4	5
6	7	8	9	10	11	12
13	14	15	16	17	18	19
20	21	22	23	24	25	26
27	28	29	30			

October

Sun	Mon	Tue	Wed	Thu	Fri	Sat
				1	2	3
4	5	6	7	8	9	10
11	12	13	14	15	16	17
18	19	20	21	22	23	24
25	26	27	28	29	30	31

November

Sun	Mon	Tue	Wed	Thu	Fri	Sat
1	2	3	4	5	6	7
8	9	10	11	12	13	14
15	16	17	18	19	20	21
22	23	24	25	26	27	28
29	30					

December

Sun	Mon	Tue	Wed	Thu	Fri	Sat
		1	2	3	4	5
6	7	8	9	10	11	12
13	14	15	16	17	18	19
20	21	22	23	24	25	26
27	28	29	30	31		

Post Office Holidays

Jan. 1, Jan. 19, Feb. 16, May 25, July 3,

Sept. 7, Oct. 12, Nov. 11, Nov. 26, Dec. 25

CALENDAR

2027

January

Sun	Mon	Tue	Wed	Thu	Fri	Sat
					1	2
3	4	5	6	7	8	9
10	11	12	13	14	15	16
17	18	19	20	21	22	23
24	25	26	27	28	29	30
31						

February

Sun	Mon	Tue	Wed	Thu	Fri	Sat
	1	2	3	4	5	6
7	8	9	10	11	12	13
14	15	16	17	18	19	20
21	22	23	24	25	26	27
28						

March

Sun	Mon	Tue	Wed	Thu	Fri	Sat
	1	2	3	4	5	6
7	8	9	10	11	12	13
14	15	16	17	18	19	20
21	22	23	24	25	26	27
28	29	30	31			

April

Sun	Mon	Tue	Wed	Thu	Fri	Sat
				1	2	3
4	5	6	7	8	9	10
11	12	13	14	15	16	17
18	19	20	21	22	23	24
25	26	27	28	29	30	

May

Sun	Mon	Tue	Wed	Thu	Fri	Sat
						1
2	3	4	5	6	7	8
9	10	11	12	13	14	15
16	17	18	19	20	21	22
23	24	25	26	27	28	29
30	31					

June

Sun	Mon	Tue	Wed	Thu	Fri	Sat
		1	2	3	4	5
6	7	8	9	10	11	12
13	14	15	16	17	18	19
20	21	22	23	24	25	26
27	28	29	30			

July

Sun	Mon	Tue	Wed	Thu	Fri	Sat
				1	2	3
4	5	6	7	8	9	10
11	12	13	14	15	16	17
18	19	20	21	22	23	24
25	26	27	28	29	30	31

August

Sun	Mon	Tue	Wed	Thu	Fri	Sat
1	2	3	4	5	6	7
8	9	10	11	12	13	14
15	16	17	18	19	20	21
22	23	24	25	26	27	28
29	30	31				

September

Sun	Mon	Tue	Wed	Thu	Fri	Sat
			1	2	3	4
5	6	7	8	9	10	11
12	13	14	15	16	17	18
19	20	21	22	23	24	25
26	27	28	29	30		

October

Sun	Mon	Tue	Wed	Thu	Fri	Sat
					1	2
3	4	5	6	7	8	9
10	11	12	13	14	15	16
17	18	19	20	21	22	23
24	25	26	27	28	29	30
31						

November

Sun	Mon	Tue	Wed	Thu	Fri	Sat
	1	2	3	4	5	6
7	8	9	10	11	12	13
14	15	16	17	18	19	20
21	22	23	24	25	26	27
28	29	30				

December

Sun	Mon	Tue	Wed	Thu	Fri	Sat
			1	2	3	4
5	6	7	8	9	10	11
12	13	14	15	16	17	18
19	20	21	22	23	24	25
26	27	28	29	30	31	

Post Office Holidays

Jan. 1, Jan. 18, Feb. 15, May 31, July 5,

Sept. 6, Oct. 11, Nov. 11, Nov. 25, Dec. 24, Dec. 31

CALENDAR

2028

January

Sun	Mon	Tue	Wed	Thu	Fri	Sat
						1
2	3	4	5	6	7	8
9	10	11	12	13	14	15
16	17	18	19	20	21	22
23	24	25	26	27	28	29
30	31					

February

Sun	Mon	Tue	Wed	Thu	Fri	Sat
		1	2	3	4	5
6	7	8	9	10	11	12
13	14	15	16	17	18	19
20	21	22	23	24	25	26
27	28	29				

March

Sun	Mon	Tue	Wed	Thu	Fri	Sat
			1	2	3	4
5	6	7	8	9	10	11
12	13	14	15	16	17	18
19	20	21	22	23	24	25
26	27	28	29	30	31	

April

Sun	Mon	Tue	Wed	Thu	Fri	Sat
						1
2	3	4	5	6	7	8
9	10	11	12	13	14	15
16	17	18	19	20	21	22
23	24	25	26	27	28	29
30						

May

Sun	Mon	Tue	Wed	Thu	Fri	Sat
	1	2	3	4	5	6
7	8	9	10	11	12	13
14	15	16	17	18	19	20
21	22	23	24	25	26	27
28	29	30	31			

June

Sun	Mon	Tue	Wed	Thu	Fri	Sat
				1	2	3
4	5	6	7	8	9	10
11	12	13	14	15	16	17
18	19	20	21	22	23	24
25	26	27	28	29	30	

July

Sun	Mon	Tue	Wed	Thu	Fri	Sat
						1
2	3	4	5	6	7	8
9	10	11	12	13	14	15
16	17	18	19	20	21	22
23	24	25	26	27	28	29
30	31					

August

Sun	Mon	Tue	Wed	Thu	Fri	Sat
		1	2	3	4	5
6	7	8	9	10	11	12
13	14	15	16	17	18	19
20	21	22	23	24	25	26
27	28	29	30	31		

September

Sun	Mon	Tue	Wed	Thu	Fri	Sat
					1	2
3	4	5	6	7	8	9
10	11	12	13	14	15	16
17	18	19	20	21	22	23
24	25	26	27	28	29	30

October

Sun	Mon	Tue	Wed	Thu	Fri	Sat
1	2	3	4	5	6	7
8	9	10	11	12	13	14
15	16	17	18	19	20	21
22	23	24	25	26	27	28
29	30	31				

November

Sun	Mon	Tue	Wed	Thu	Fri	Sat
			1	2	3	4
5	6	7	8	9	10	11
12	13	14	15	16	17	18
19	20	21	22	23	24	25
26	27	28	29	30		

December

Sun	Mon	Tue	Wed	Thu	Fri	Sat
					1	2
3	4	5	6	7	8	9
10	11	12	13	14	15	16
17	18	19	20	21	22	23
24	25	26	27	28	29	30
31						

Post Office Holidays

Jan. 1, Jan. 17, Feb. 21, May 29, July 4,

Sept. 4, Oct. 9, Nov. 10, Nov. 23, Dec. 25

CALENDAR

2029

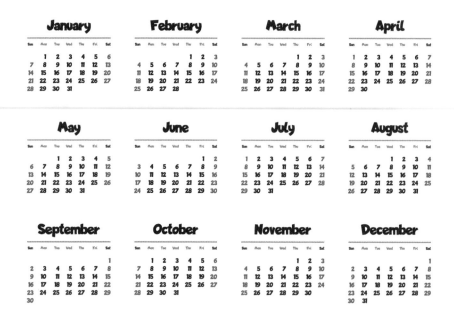

January

Sun	Mon	Tue	Wed	Thu	Fri	Sat
	1	2	3	4	5	6
7	8	9	10	11	12	13
14	15	16	17	18	19	20
21	22	23	24	25	26	27
28	29	30	31			

February

Sun	Mon	Tue	Wed	Thu	Fri	Sat
				1	2	3
4	5	6	7	8	9	10
11	12	13	14	15	16	17
18	19	20	21	22	23	24
25	26	27	28			

March

Sun	Mon	Tue	Wed	Thu	Fri	Sat
				1	2	3
4	5	6	7	8	9	10
11	12	13	14	15	16	17
18	19	20	21	22	23	24
25	26	27	28	29	30	31

April

Sun	Mon	Tue	Wed	Thu	Fri	Sat
1	2	3	4	5	6	7
8	9	10	11	12	13	14
15	16	17	18	19	20	21
22	23	24	25	26	27	28
29	30					

May

Sun	Mon	Tue	Wed	Thu	Fri	Sat
		1	2	3	4	5
6	7	8	9	10	11	12
13	14	15	16	17	18	19
20	21	22	23	24	25	26
27	28	29	30	31		

June

Sun	Mon	Tue	Wed	Thu	Fri	Sat
					1	2
3	4	5	6	7	8	9
10	11	12	13	14	15	16
17	18	19	20	21	22	23
24	25	26	27	28	29	30

July

Sun	Mon	Tue	Wed	Thu	Fri	Sat
1	2	3	4	5	6	7
8	9	10	11	12	13	14
15	16	17	18	19	20	21
22	23	24	25	26	27	28
29	30	31				

August

Sun	Mon	Tue	Wed	Thu	Fri	Sat
			1	2	3	4
5	6	7	8	9	10	11
12	13	14	15	16	17	18
19	20	21	22	23	24	25
26	27	28	29	30	31	

September

Sun	Mon	Tue	Wed	Thu	Fri	Sat
						1
2	3	4	5	6	7	8
9	10	11	12	13	14	15
16	17	18	19	20	21	22
23	24	25	26	27	28	29
30						

October

Sun	Mon	Tue	Wed	Thu	Fri	Sat
	1	2	3	4	5	6
7	8	9	10	11	12	13
14	15	16	17	18	19	20
21	22	23	24	25	26	27
28	29	30	31			

November

Sun	Mon	Tue	Wed	Thu	Fri	Sat
				1	2	3
4	5	6	7	8	9	10
11	12	13	14	15	16	17
18	19	20	21	22	23	24
25	26	27	28	29	30	

December

Sun	Mon	Tue	Wed	Thu	Fri	Sat
						1
2	3	4	5	6	7	8
9	10	11	12	13	14	15
16	17	18	19	20	21	22
23	24	25	26	27	28	29
30	31					

Post Office Holidays

Jan 1, Jan 15, Feb 19, May 28, Jul 4,

Sep 3, Oct 8, Nov 12, Nov 22, Dec 25

Taking care of the Pacific Crest Trail is a full-time effort.

The Pacific Crest Trail Association's mission is to protect, preserve and promote the trail as a resource for hikers and equestrians and for the value that wild lands provide to all people.

Through a formal partnership with the U.S. Forest Service, our nonprofit membership organization is the primary caretaker of this 2,650-mile National Scenic Trail as it winds through the American West's most beautiful landscapes.

Each year, PCTA volunteers and paid staff members clear downed trees and repair washed out tread. We monitor threats to the trail and speak up on its behalf. We tell the trail's story in print and online. And we advocate for federal support by visiting our elected leaders in Washington, D.C.

All this effort safeguards the experiences and solitude people deserve when they venture into the wild.

Please help preserve this national treasure for future generations by joining the PCTA.

Your $35 annual membership will ensure that this trail will never end.

1331 Garden Highway, Suite 230
Sacramento, CA 95833

916-285-1846

www.pcta.org • info@pcta.org

Pacific Crest Trail
Association

PACIFIC CREST TRAIL ASSOCIATION

All the proceeds of this book will be donated by the author to the Jane and Flicka Endowment Fund. Jane and Flicka were two hikers who lost their lives on a thru-hike of the PCT when a car struck them on the highway near the end of their journey. They were returning to the trail after a stop in a nearby town for supplies.

Family and friends established this endowment fund in their memory to benefit the PCTA and to keep their spirit alive along the trail. This fund is used to maintain the Pacific Crest National Scenic Trail and promote its use by individuals from around the world.

A message from Barbara Perry, Flicka's mother:

I have walked the highway where Jane and Flicka died. We considered putting a memorial up for them, to join the others, yet we did not want to remember or memorialize that place. We wanted to think of them out on the trail, in God's country, and so we chose their memorial to be the Jane and Flicka Endowment Fund for the PCTA—something that will live forever and help to preserve the trail for others to be inspired.

Flicka and Jane always knew, way beyond their years, exactly how precious life is, which is one reason they touched so many in their lives and their death. In Flicka's last journal were words from Henry David Thoreau: "I went to the woods because I wished to live deliberately, to front only the essential facts of life, and see if I could not learn what it had to teach, and not, when I came to die, discover that I had not lived. Living is so dear."

The Jane and Flicka Endowment Fund was created to help preserve and protect the trail by providing a foundation for the PCTA. The spirit of Jane and Flicka continues to inspire all of us in ways great and small.

If you would like to contribute to the fund, please send donations to the PCTA, referencing "Jane and Flicka Endowment Fund" on the check.

ぼくの 最愛の もの、   *My Beloved,*
これが 全部 夢 ならば、   *If this is all a dream,*
ああ、目覚めたくはなし。   *Then, I do not want to wake up.*

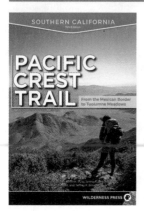
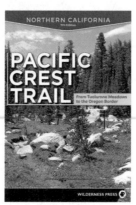

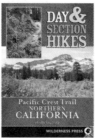
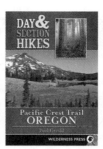
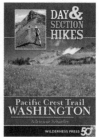